PSYCHOLOGY AND RELIGION

Based on the Terry Lectures delivered at Yale University

PSYCHOLOGY

AND

RELIGION

BY

CARL GUSTAV JUNG, M.D.

NEW HAVEN AND LONDON
YALE UNIVERSITY PRESS

Printed in the United States of America by
The Vail-Ballou Press, Inc., Binghamton, New York.
ISBN: 0–300–00613–6 (cloth)
         0–300–00137–1 (paper)

46   45   44   43   42   41   40

CONTENTS

I

THE AUTONOMY OF THE
UNCONSCIOUS MIND

AS it seems to be the intention of the founder of the Terry Lectures to enable representatives of science, as well as of philosophy and of other spheres of human knowledge, to contribute to the discussion of the eternal problem of religion, and since Yale University has bestowed upon me the great honor of delivering the Terry Lectures of 1937, I assume that it will be my task to show what psychology, or rather that special branch of medical psychology which I represent, has to do with or to say about religion. Since religion is incontestably one of the earliest and most universal activities of the human mind, it is self-evident that any kind of psychology which touches upon the psychological structure of human personality cannot avoid at least observing the fact that religion is not only a sociological or historical phenomenon, but also something of considerable personal concern to a great number of individuals.

Notwithstanding the fact that I have often been called a philosopher, I am an empiricist and adhere to the phenomenological standpoint. I trust that it does not collide with the principles of scientific empiricism if one occasionally makes certain reflections which go beyond a mere accumulation and classification of experience. As a matter of fact I believe that an experience is not even possible without reflection, because "experience" is a process of assimilation, without which there could be no understanding. As this statement indicates, I approach psychological matters from a scientific and not from a philosophical standpoint. In as much as religion has a very important psychological aspect, I am dealing with it from a purely empirical point of view, that is, I restrict myself to the observation of phenomena and I refrain from any application of metaphysical or philosophical considerations. I do not deny the validity of other considerations, but I cannot claim to be competent to apply them correctly. I am aware that most people believe they know all there is to be known about psychology, because they think that psychology is nothing but what they know of themselves. But I am afraid psychology is a good deal more than that. While having little to do with philosophy, it has much to do with empirical facts, many of which are not easily accessible to the average experience. It is my intention in this book to give a few glimpses, at least, of the way in which practical psychology becomes confronted with the problem of religion. It is self-evident that the vastness of the problem requires far more than three lectures, as the necessary demonstration of concrete detail needs a great deal of time as well as of explanation. My first chapter will be a sort of introduction to the problem of practical psychology and religion. The second is concerned with facts which bear out the existence of an authentic religious function in the unconscious mind. The third deals with religious symbolism by unconscious processes.

Since I am going to present a rather unusual argument, I cannot assume that my audience is completely aware of the methodological standpoint of that kind of psychology which I represent. This standpoint is exclusively phenomenological, that is, it is concerned with occurrences, events, experiences, in a word, with facts. Its truth is a fact and not a judgment. Speaking for instance of the motive of the virgin birth, psychology is only concerned with the fact that there is such an idea, but it is not concerned with the question whether such an idea is true or false in any other sense. It is psychologically true in as much as it exists. Psychological existence is subjective in so far as an idea occurs in only one individual. But it is objective in so far as it is established by a society—by a consensus gentium.

This point of view is the same as that of natural science. Psychology deals with ideas and other mental contents as zoology for instance deals with different species of animals. An elephant is true because it exists. The elephant, moreover, is neither a conclusion nor a statement nor a subjective judgment of a creator. It is a phenomenon. But we are so used to the idea that psychical events are wilful and arbitrary products, even inventions of the human creator, that we can hardly liberate ourselves from the prejudiced

view that the psyche and its contents are nothing but
our own arbitrary invention or the more or less illu-
sory product of assumption and judgment. The fact
is that certain ideas exist almost everywhere and at
all times and they can even spontaneously create
themselves quite apart from migration and tradition.
They are not made by the individual, but they rather
happen—they even force themselves upon the individual's consciousness. This is not platonic philosophy but empirical psychology.

In speaking of religion I must make clear from the
start what I mean by that term. Religion, as the
Latin word denotes, is a careful and scrupulous observation of what Rudolf Otto[1] aptly termed the
"numinosum," that is, a dynamic existence or effect,
not caused by an arbitrary act of will. On the contrary, it seizes and controls the human subject, which
is always rather its victim than its creator. The numinosum is an involuntary condition of the subject,
whatever its cause may be. At all events, religious
teaching as well as the consensus gentium always and
everywhere explains this condition as being due to a
cause external to the individual. The numinosum is
either a quality of a visible object or the influence of
an invisible presence causing a peculiar alteration of
consciousness. This is, at least, the general rule.

There are, however, certain exceptions when it
comes to the question of practice or ritual. A great
many ritualistic performances are carried out for the
sole purpose of producing at will the effect of the

numinosum by certain devices of a magic nature, such as invocation, incantation, sacrifice, meditation and other yoga practices, self-inflicted tortures of various descriptions and so forth. But a religious belief in an external and objective divine cause always precedes any such performance. The Catholic church, for instance, administers the sacraments with the purpose of bestowing their spiritual blessings upon the believer; but since this act would amount to enforcing the presence of divine grace by an indubitably magic procedure, it is logically argued that nobody is able to compel divine grace to be present in the sacramental act, but that it is nevertheless inevitably present, the sacrament being a divine institution which God would not have caused to be if he had not had it in mind to support it.[2]

Religion appears to me to be a peculiar attitude of the human mind, which could be formulated in accordance with the original use of the term "religio," that is, a careful consideration and observation of certain dynamic factors, understood to be "powers," spirits, demons, gods, laws, ideas, ideals or whatever name man has given to such factors as he has found in his world powerful, dangerous or helpful enough to be taken into careful consideration, or grand, beautiful and meaningful enough to be devoutly adored and loved. In colloquial language one often says of somebody who is enthusiastically interested in a certain pursuit, that he is almost "religiously devoted" to his cause; William James, for instance, remarks that a scientist often has no creed, but "his temper is devout."[3]

I want to make clear that by the term "religion"[4] I do not mean a creed. It is, however, true that on the one hand every confession is originally based upon the experience of the numinosum and on the other hand upon Πίστις, the loyalty, trust, and confidence toward a definitely experienced numinous effect and the subsequent alteration of consciousness: the conversion of Paul is a striking example of this. "Religion," it might be said, is the term that designates the attitude peculiar to a consciousness which has been altered by the experience of the numinosum.

Creeds are codified and dogmatized forms of original religious experience.[5] The contents of the experience have become sanctified and usually congealed in a rigid, often elaborate, structure. The practice and the reproduction of the original experience have become a ritual and an unchangeable institution. This does not necessarily mean a lifeless petrification. On the contrary it can become the form of religious experience for ages of time and for millions of people without there being any vital necessity for alterations. Although the Catholic church has often been blamed for a particular rigidity, it admits nevertheless that the dogma has its life and hence is capable of undergoing change and development. Even the number of dogmas is unlimited and can be augmented in the course of time. The same holds true of the ritual. Yet all changes and developments are confined within the frame of the originally experienced facts, thereby involving a particular kind of dogmatic content and emotional value. Even Protestantism—which has surrendered apparently to an almost unlimited liberation from dogmatic tradition and from codified ritual and has thus split into more than four hundred denominations—even Protestantism is bound at least to be Christian and to express itself within the frame of the conviction that God has revealed himself in Christ, who suffered for mankind. This is a definite frame, with definite contents, which cannot be coupled with or amplified by Buddhistic or Islamic ideas and emotions. Yet it is unquestionable that not only Buddha or Mohammed or Confucius or Zarathustra represents religious phenomena, but that Mithras, Attis, Kybele, Mani, Hermes and many exotic cults do so as well. The psychologist, in as much as he assumes a scientific attitude, has to disregard the claim of every creed to be the unique and eternal truth. He must keep his eye on the human side of the religious problem, in that he is concerned with the original religious experience quite apart from what the creeds have made of it.

Being a doctor and a specialist in nervous and mental diseases my point of departure is not any creed, but the psychology of the homo religiosus, the man who takes into account and carefully observes certain factors which influence him and, through him, his general condition. It is easy to denominate and define those factors according to historical tradition or anthropological knowledge, but to do the same thing from the standpoint of psychology is an uncommonly difficult task. What I can contribute to the question of religion is derived entirely from my practical experience, both with my patients and with so-called normal beings. As our experience with people depends considerably upon what we do with them, I can see no other way of proceeding than to give you at least a general idea of the line I take in my professional work.

Since every neurosis is connected with man's most intimate life, there will always be some hesitation when a patient has to give a complete account of all the circumstances and complications which have originally led him into a morbid condition. But why shouldn't he be able to talk freely? Why should he be afraid or shy or prudish? The reason is that he is "carefully observing" certain external factors which form important constituents of what one calls public opinion or respectability or reputation. And even if he trusts his doctor, and if he is no longer shy of him, he will be reluctant or even afraid to admit certain things to *himself*, as if it were dangerous to become conscious of himself. One is usually afraid of things which seem to be overpowering. But is there anything in man that is stronger than himself? We should not forget that any neurosis means a corresponding amount of demoralization. In so far as man is neurotic, he has lost confidence in himself. A neurosis is a humiliating defeat and is felt as such by people who are not entirely unconscious of their own psychology. And one is defeated by something "unreal." Doctors may have assured the patient, long ago, that there is nothing the matter with him, that he does not suffer from a real heart disease or from a real cancer. His symptoms are quite imaginary. The more he believes that he is a "malade imaginaire," the more a feeling of inferiority permeates his whole personality. "If my symptoms are imaginary," he will say, "where have I caught such a confounded imagination and why should I cherish such a perfect nuisance?" It is indeed pathetic to have an intelligent man almost imploringly assure you that he is suffering from an intestinal cancer and declare at the same time in a despondent voice that of course he knows his cancer to be a merely imaginary affair.

Our usual materialistic conception of the psyche is, I am afraid, not particularly helpful in neurotic cases. If only the soul were endowed with a subtle body, then one could say, at least, that this breath or smoke body was suffering from a real though somewhat airy cancer, in much the same way as the gross material body could be subject to a similar ailment. There would, at least, be something real. Medicine therefore feels a strong dislike toward anything of a psychical nature—either the body is ill or there is nothing the matter. And if you cannot prove that the body is really diseased, that is because our present means do not enable the physician to find the true nature of the undoubtedly organic trouble.

But what is the psyche after all? A materialistic prejudice explains it as a merely epiphenomenal by-product of organic processes in the brain. Any psychic disturbance must be an organic or physical disorder which is undiscoverable only because of the insufficiency of our actual diagnostic means. The undeniable connection between psyche and brain gives this point of view a certain strength, but not enough to make it an unshakable truth. We do not know whether there is a real disturbance of the organic processes of the brain in a case of neurosis, and if there are disorders of an endocrine nature it is impossible to say whether they are not effects rather than causes.

On the other hand it is indubitable that the real causes of neuroses are psychological. It is indeed very difficult to imagine that an organic or physical disorder can be cured in a moment by a mere confession. But I have seen a case of hysterical fever, with a temperature as high as 102°, which was cured in a few minutes by a confession of the psychological cause. And how should we explain cases of manifest physical diseases that are influenced and even cured by a mere discussion of certain painful psychological conflicts? I have seen a case of psoriasis, extending practically over the whole body, which was reduced by nine-tenths after a few weeks of psychological treatment. In another case, a patient had recently undergone an operation for distention of the colon, forty centimeters of which had been removed, but this was fol-

lowed by another extraordinary distention of the
colon. The patient was desperate and refused to per-
mit a second operation, though the surgeon thought
it indispensable. As soon as certain intimate psychological facts were discovered, the colon began to function normally.

Such experiences, which are by no means rare,
make it exceedingly difficult to believe that the psyche is nothing, or that an imaginary fact is unreal. It
is only not there where a nearsighted mind seeks it.
It is existent but not in a physical form. It is an almost ridiculous prejudice to assume that existence
can only be physical. As a matter of fact the only
form of existence we know of immediately is psychic.
We might well say, on the contrary, that physical
existence is merely an inference, since we know of
matter only in so far as we perceive psychic images
transmitted by the senses.

We are surely making a great mistake when we
forget this simple yet fundamental truth. If a neurosis should have no other cause at all than imagination, it would, none the less, be a very real thing. If
a man imagined that I was his arch-enemy and killed
me, I should be dead on account of mere imagination.
Imaginations do exist and they may be just as real
and just as obnoxious or dangerous as physical conditions. I even believe that psychical dangers are
much more dangerous than epidemics or earthquakes.
Not even the medieval epidemics of bubonic plague
or smallpox killed as many people as certain differ-

ences of opinion in 1914 or certain political ideals in Russia.

Although our mind cannot grasp its own form of existence, owing to the lack of the Archimedean point outside, it nevertheless exists. Psyche is existent, it is even existence itself.

What shall we now reply to our patient with the imaginary cancer? I would tell him: "Yes, my friend, you are really suffering from a cancer-like thing, you really harbor a deadly evil which, however, will not kill your body, because it is imaginary. But it will eventually kill your soul. It has already spoilt and has even poisoned your human relations and your personal happiness and it will go on thus ever increasing until it has swallowed your whole psychic existence. So that in the end you will not be human any more, but will be an evil destructive tumor."

It is obvious to our man that he is not the originator of his morbid imagination, although his theoretical mind will certainly suggest that he is the owner and maker of his own imagination. If one is suffering from a real cancer, one never believes oneself to be the responsible originator of such an evil, despite the fact that the cancer is in one's own body. But when it comes to the psyche we instantly feel a kind of responsibility, as if we were the makers of our psychical conditions. This prejudice is of relatively recent date. Not very long ago even highly civilized people believed that psychic agencies could influence our mind and feeling. There were ghosts, wizards and witches, demons and angels, and even gods, that could produce certain psychological alterations in man. In former times the man with the idea that he had cancer might have felt quite differently about his idea. He would probably have assumed that somebody had worked witchcraft against him or that he was possessed. He never would have thought himself to be the originator of such a phantasy.

As a matter of fact I assume that his cancer idea is a spontaneous growth, originating in that part of the psyche which is not identical with consciousness. It appears to be an autonomous development intruding upon consciousness. Of consciousness one might say that it is our own psychical existence, but the cancer is *its* own psychical existence, independent of ourselves. This statement seems to formulate the observable facts completely. If we submit such a case to an association experiment,[6] we soon discover that the man is not master in his own house. His reactions will be delayed, altered, suppressed or replaced by autonomous intruders. There will be a number of stimulus words which cannot be answered by his conscious intention. They will be answered by certain autonomous contents, which are very often unconscious even to the test person. In our case we will certainly discover answers which come from the psychic complex at the root of the cancer idea. Whenever a stimulus word touches something connected with the hidden complex, the reaction of the ego consciousness will be disturbed, or even replaced, by an answer coming from the complex. It is just as if the complex were an autonomous being capable of interfering with the intentions of the ego. Complexes indeed behave like secondary or partial personalities in possession of a mental life of their own.

Many complexes are merely split from consciousness because the latter preferred to get rid of them by repression. But there are others that have never been in consciousness before and that therefore could never have been arbitrarily repressed. They grow out of the unconscious mind and invade consciousness with their weird and unassailable convictions and impulses. Our patient's case belonged in the latter category. Despite his culture and intelligence, he was a helpless victim of something which obsessed or possessed him. He was utterly unable to help himself in any way against the demoniacal power of his morbid idea. It overgrew him indeed like a carcinoma. One day the idea had appeared and from then on it remained unshakably; there were only short free intervals.

The existence of such cases explains, to a certain extent, why people are afraid of becoming conscious of themselves. There might really be something behind the screen—one never knows—and thus people prefer "to take into account and to observe carefully" factors external to their consciousness. In most people there is a sort of primitive δεισιδαιμονία concerning the possible contents of the unconscious. Beyond all natural shyness, shame and tact, there is a secret fear of the unknown "perils of the soul." Of course one is reluctant to admit such a ridiculous fear. But one should realize that this fear is by no means unjustifiable; on the contrary, it is only too well founded. We are never sure that a new idea will not seize either upon ourselves or upon our neighbors. We know from modern as well as from ancient history that such ideas can be rather strange, so peculiar, indeed, that not everybody can agree with them. The result may be that all dissenters, no matter how well meaning or reasonable they are, get burnt alive or have their heads cut off or are disposed of in masses by the more modern machine gun. We cannot even calm ourselves with the idea that such things belong to a remote past. Unfortunately they seem to belong not only to the present moment, but, quite particularly, to the future. "Homo homini lupus" is a sad, yet eternal truism. There is indeed reason enough why man should be afraid of those nonpersonal forces dwelling in the unconscious mind. We are blissfully unconscious of those forces because they never, or almost never, appear in our personal dealings and under ordinary circumstances. But if, on the other hand, people crowd together and form a mob, then the dynamics of the collective man are set free—beasts or demons which lie dormant in every person till he is part of a mob. Man in the crowd is unconsciously lowered to an inferior moral and intellectual level, to that level which is always there, below the threshold of consciousness, ready to break forth as soon as it is stimulated through the formation of a crowd.

It is, to my mind, a fatal mistake to consider the human psyche as a merely personal affair and to explain it exclusively from a personal point of view. Such a mode of explanation is only applicable to the individual in his ordinary everyday occupations and relationships. If, however, some slight trouble occurs, perhaps in the form of an unforeseen and somewhat extraordinary event, instantly instinctive forces are called up, forces which appear to be wholly unexpected, new, and even strange. They can no longer be explained by personal motives, being comparable rather to certain primitive occurrences like panics at solar eclipses and such things. To explain the murderous outburst of Bolshevistic ideas by a personal father complex appears to me as singularly inadequate.

The change of character that is brought about by the uprush of collective forces is amazing. A gentle and reasonable being can be transformed into a maniac or a savage beast. One is always inclined to lay the blame on external circumstances, but nothing could explode in us if it had not been there. As a matter of fact, we are always living upon a volcano and there is, as far as we know, no human means of protection against a possible outburst which will destroy everybody within its reach. It is certainly a good thing to preach reason and common sense, but what if your audience is a lunatic asylum or a crowd in a collective seizure? There is not much difference either, because the madman as well as the mob is moved by nonpersonal, overwhelming forces.

As a matter of fact, it needs as little as a neurosis to conjure up a force that cannot be dealt with by reasonable means. Our cancer case shows clearly how impotent human reason and intellect are against the most palpable nonsense. I always advise my patients to take such obvious but invincible nonsense as the manifestation of a power and a meaning not yet understood. Experience has taught me that it is a much more effective method of procedure to take such a fact seriously and to seek for a suitable explanation. But an explanation is suitable only when it produces a hypothesis equal to the morbid effect. Our case is confronted with a will power and a suggestion more than equal to anything his consciousness can put against it. In this precarious situation it would be bad strategy to convince the patient that he is somehow, though in a highly incomprehensible way, at the back of his own symptom, secretly inventing and supporting it. Such a suggestion would instantly paralyze his fighting spirit, and he would get demoralized. It is much better if he understands that his complex is an autonomous power directed against his conscious personality. Moreover, such an explanation fits the actual facts much better than a reduction to personal motives. An apparent personal motivation does exist, but it is not made by intention, it just happens to the patient.

When in the Babylonian Epos Gilgamesh's arro-

gance and ὕβρις defy the gods, they invent and create a man equal in strength to Gilgamesh in order to
check the hero's unlawful ambition. The very same
thing has happened to our patient: he is a thinker
who has settled, or is always going to settle, the world
by the power of his intellect and reason. His ambition
has at least succeeded in carving his own personal
fate. He has forced everything under the inexorable
law of his reason, but somewhere nature escaped and
came back with a vengeance in the form of perfectly
unassailable nonsense, the cancer idea. This clever device was formed by the unconscious mind to keep him
on a merciless and cruel leash. It was the worst blow
which could be given to all his reasonable ideals and
above all to his belief in the all-powerful human will.
Such an obsession can only occur in a person who
makes a habitual misuse of reason and intellect for an
egotistical power purpose.

Gilgamesh, however, escaped the revenge of the
gods. He had warning dreams to which he paid attention. They showed him how he could overcome his
foe. Our patient, living in an age where the gods have
become extinct and are even in bad repute, also had
such dreams, but he did not listen to them. How could
an intelligent man be so superstitious as to take
dreams seriously! The very common prejudice against
dreams is but one of the symptoms of a far more serious undervaluation of the human soul in general. The
marvelous development of science and technics has
been counterbalanced on the other side by an appall-

ing lack of wisdom and introspection. It is true that our religious teaching speaks of an immortal soul; but it has very few kind words for the actual human psyche, which would go straight to eternal damnation if it were not for a special act of Divine Grace. Those two important factors are largely responsible for the general undervaluation of the psyche, but not entirely. Much older than those relatively recent developments are the primitive fear of and aversion to everything that borders on the unconscious.

Consciousness must have been a very precarious thing in its beginnings. In relatively primitive societies we can still observe how easily consciousness is lost. One of the "perils of the soul"[7] is, for instance, the loss of a soul. This is a case of a part of the psyche becoming unconscious again. Another example is the amok condition,[8] the equivalent of the berserk condition in the Germanic saga.[9] This is a more or less complete trance, often accompanied by devastating social effects. Even an ordinary emotion can cause a considerable loss of consciousness. Primitives therefore cherish elaborate forms of politeness, speaking with a hushed voice, laying down their weapons, crouching, bowing the head, showing the palms. Even our own forms of politeness still show a "religious" observation of possible psychical dangers. We propitiate the fates by wishing magically a good day. It is not good form to keep the left hand in your pocket or behind your back when shaking hands. If you want to be particularly propitiating you use both hands. Before people of great authority we bow with uncovered head, i.e., we offer our head unprotected, in order to propitiate the powerful one, who might quite easily fall suddenly a prey to a fit of uncontrollable violence. In war dances primitives can become so excited that they may shed blood.

The life of the primitive is filled with constant regard for the ever-lurking possibility of psychical dangers, and the attempts and procedures employed to diminish the risks are very numerous. The creation of tabooed areas is an external evidence of this fact. The innumerable taboos are delimited psychical areas, meticulously and fearfully observed. I made a terrific mistake once when I was with a tribe on the southern slopes of Mt. Elgon. I wanted to inquire about the ghost houses I frequently found in the woods and during a palaver I mentioned the word "seleteni" meaning "ghost." Instantly everybody was silent and painfully embarrassed. They all looked away from me because I had spoken aloud a carefully hushed-up word, and had thus invited most dangerous consequences. I had to change the subject in order to be able to continue the meeting. The same men assured me that they never had dreams; they were the prerogative of the chief and of the medicine man. The medicine man then confessed to me that he no longer had any dreams, for they had the District Commissioner now instead. "Since the English are in the country we have no dreams any more," he said. "The District Commissioner knows everything about war

and diseases, and about where we have got to live."
This strange statement is based upon the fact that
dreams were formerly the supreme political guide, the
voice of "mungu." Therefore it would have been un-
wise for an ordinary man to suggest that he had
dreams.

Dreams are the voice of the Unknown, that ever
threatens with new schemes, new dangers, sacrifices,
warfare and other troublesome things. An African
negro once dreamt that his enemies had taken him
prisoner and burnt him alive. The next day he called
his relatives together and implored them to burn him.
They consented to do so to the extent that they bound
his feet together and put them in the fire. He was of
course badly crippled but had escaped his foes.[10]

There are any amount of creeds and ceremonies
that exist for the sole purpose of forming a defense
against the unexpected, dangerous tendencies of the
unconscious. The peculiar fact that the dream is the
divine voice and messenger and yet an unending
source of trouble, does not disturb the primitive
mind. We still find obvious remnants of this primitive
fact in the psychology of the Jewish prophets.[11]
Often enough they hesitate to listen to the voice. And
it was, we must admit, rather hard on a pious man
like Hosea to marry the prostitute in order to obey
the Lord's command. Since the dawn of mankind
there has been a marked tendency to delimit the un-
ruly and arbitrary "supernatural" influence by definite forms and laws. And this process has gone on in

history by the multiplication of rites, institutions and creeds. In the last two thousand years we find the institution of the Christian church assuming a mediating and protective function between these influences and man. It is not denied in medieval ecclesiastical writings that a divine influx could take place in dreams, for instance, but this view is not exactly encouraged and the church reserves the right to decide whether a revelation is to be considered authentic or not.[12] In spite of the fact that the church recognizes the undeniable emanation of certain dreams from God, it is disinclined, even positively averse, to any serious occupation with dreams, while admitting that some might contain an immediate revelation. Thus the change in mental attitudes which has taken place in recent centuries is, from this point of view at least, not wholly unwelcome to the church, because it has effectively discouraged the former introspective attitude which was favorable to a serious consideration of dreams and inner experiences.

Protestantism, having pulled down many a wall which had been carefully erected by the church, began immediately to experience the disintegrating and schismatic effect of individual revelation. As soon as the dogmatic fence was broken down and as soon as the ritual had lost the authority of its efficiency, man was confronted with an inner experience, without the protection and the guidance of a dogma and a ritual which are the unparalleled quintessence of Christian as well as of pagan religious experience. Protestantism has, in the main, lost all the finer shades of the dogma: the mass, the confession, the greater part of the liturgy and the sacrificial importance of priesthood.

I must emphasize the point that this statement is not a judgment of values and has no intention of being one. I merely state the facts. Protestantism has, however, intensified the authority of the Bible as a substitute for the lost authority of the church. But as history has shown, one can interpret certain biblical texts in many ways. Nor has the scientific criticism of the New Testament been very helpful in enhancing the divine character of the holy writings. It is also a fact that under the influence of a so-called scientific enlightenment great masses of educated people have either left the church or have become profoundly indifferent to it. If they were all dull rationalists or neurotic intellectuals the loss would not be regrettable. But many of them are religious people, only incapable of agreeing with the actually existing forms of creed. If this were not so, one could hardly explain the remarkable effect of the Buchman movement on the more or less educated Protestant classes. The Catholic who has turned his back on the church usually develops a secret or manifest inclination toward atheism, whereas the Protestant follows, if possible, a sectarian movement. The absolutism of the Catholic church seems to demand an equally absolute negation, while Protestant relativism permits variations.

It may perhaps be thought that I have gone a bit far
into the history of Christianity for no other purpose
than to explain the prejudice against dreams and individual inner experience. But what I have just said
might have been a part of my conversation with our
cancer patient. I told him that it would be better to
take his obsession seriously instead of reviling it as
pathological nonsense. But to take it seriously would
mean acknowledging it as a sort of diagnostic information of the fact that, in a psyche which really existed, trouble had arisen in the form of a cancer-like
growth. "But," he will certainly ask, "what could
that growth be?" And I shall answer: "I do not
know," as indeed I do not. Although, as I mentioned
before, it is surely a compensatory or complementary
unconscious development, nothing is yet known about
its specific nature or about its content. It is a spontaneous manifestation of the unconscious mind, based
upon contents which are not to be found in consciousness.

My patient is now very curious how I shall set
about getting at those contents which form the root
of the obsession. I then inform him, at the risk of
shocking him severely, that his dreams will provide us
with all the necessary information. We will take them
as if they issued from an intelligent, purposive and,
as it were, personal source. This is of course a bold
hypothesis and at the same time an adventure, because we are going to give extraordinary credit to a

discreditable entity, whose very existence is still denied by not a few contemporary psychologists as well as by philosophers. A famous anthropologist, to whom I had demonstrated my way of proceeding, made the typical remark: "That's all very interesting indeed, but dangerous." Yes, I admit, it is dangerous, just as dangerous as a neurosis. When you want to cure a neurosis, you have to risk something. To do something without risk is merely ineffectual, as we know only too well. A surgical operation for cancer is a risk too and yet it is what has to be done. For the sake of a better understanding I have often felt tempted to advise my patients to conceive of the psyche as of a subtle body, in which subtle tumors can grow. The prejudiced belief that the psyche is unimaginable and consequently less than air or that it is a more or less philosophic system of logical concepts, is so great that, when people are not conscious of certain contents, they assume that they do not exist. There is no confidence and no belief in a reliable psychical functioning outside consciousness, and dreams are thought to be only ridiculous. Under such conditions my proposal arouses the worst suspicions. And indeed I have heard every conceivable argument under the sun that man has ever invented used against the vague specters of dreams.

Yet in dreams we find, without any profound analysis, the same conflicts and complexes whose existence can also be ascertained by the association test. Moreover, those complexes form an integral part of the existing neurosis. We have, therefore, reason to believe that dreams can give us at least as much information about the content of a neurosis as the association test. As a matter of fact they give very much more. The symptom is like the shoot above ground, yet the main plant is an extended rhizoma underground. The rhizoma represents the content of a neurosis; it is the matrix of complexes, of symptoms and of dreams. We have every reason, even, to believe that dreams mirror exactly the underground processes of the psyche. And if we get there, we literally get at the "roots" of the disease.

As it is not my intention to go further into the psychopathology of neuroses, I propose to choose another case as an example of how dreams reveal the unknown inner facts of the psyche and of what these facts consist. The dreamer is also an intellectual, of remarkable intelligence and learning. He was neurotic and was seeking my help because he felt that his neurosis had become overpowering and was slowly but surely undermining his morale. Fortunately his intellectual integrity had not yet suffered and he had the free use of his fine intelligence. On account of that I set him the task of observing and recording his dreams himself. The dreams were not analyzed or explained to him and it was only very much later that we began with their analysis. Thus the dreams I am going to demonstrate have not been tampered with at all. They represent an entirely uninfluenced natural sequence of events. The patient had never read psychology, not to speak of analytical psychology.

Since the series consists of over four hundred dreams, I could not possibly give an impression of the whole material; but I have published a selection of seventy-four of these dreams containing motives of a peculiar religious interest.[18] The dreamer, it should be said, is a Catholic by education, but he is no longer a practicing one, nor is he interested in religious problems. He belongs to those intellectuals or scientists who would be simply amazed if anybody should saddle them with religious views of any kind. If one holds that the unconscious mind is a psychical existence independent of consciousness, a case such as that of our dreamer might be of particular interest, provided we are not mistaken in our opinion about the religious character of certain dreams. And if one lays stress on the conscious mind alone and does not credit the unconscious with an independent existence, it will be interesting to find out whether or not the dream has really derived its material from conscious contents. Should the facts be in favor of the hypothesis which includes the unconscious, one can use dreams as sources of information about the possible religious tendencies of the unconscious mind.

One cannot expect that dreams will manifestly speak of religion as we know it. There are, however, just two dreams among the four hundred that obviously deal with religion. I will now give the text which the dreamer himself had taken down.

"There are many houses which have a theatrical character, a sort of stage scenery. Somebody mentions the name of Bernard Shaw. It is also mentioned that the play which is to follow refers to a remote future. One of the houses is distinguished by a signboard with the following inscription:

This is the universal Catholic church.
It is the church of the Lord.
All those who feel themselves to be instruments of the
    Lord may enter.

And below in smaller letters:

The church is founded by Jesus and Paul

—it is as if a firm boasted of its old standing. I say to my friend: 'Let us go in and have a look.' He replies: 'I do not see why many people should be together in order to have religious feelings.' But I say: 'You are a Protestant so you will never understand it.' There is a woman nodding approval. I now become aware of a bill posted on the wall of the church. It reads as follows:

'Soldiers!

'When you feel that you are under the power of the Lord avoid talking directly to him. The Lord is not accessible to words. We also recommend urgently that you should not indulge in discussions about the attributes of the Lord among yourselves. It would be fruitless, as anything of value and importance is ineffable.

'Signed: Pope . . .' (The name, however, is
                not decipherable.)

"We now enter the church. The interior resembles a mosque rather than a church, as a matter of fact it is particularly like the Hagia Sophia. There are no chairs, which produces a wonderful effect of space. There are also no images. There are only framed sentences on the walls (like those in the Hagia Sophia). One of these sentences reads: 'Do not flatter your benefactor.' The same woman who nodded approval to me before begins to weep and says: 'Then there is nothing left at all.' I reply: 'I think that it is perfectly all right,' but she vanishes.

"At first I am right in front of a pillar which obliterates the view, then I change my position and I see a crowd of people in front of me. I do not belong to them and I am standing alone. But I see them clearly and I also see their faces. They pronounce the following words: 'We confess that we are under the power of the Lord. The Kingdom of Heaven is within ourselves.' They repeat this thrice in a most solemn way. Then the organ plays a fugue by Bach and a choir sings. Sometimes it is music alone, sometimes the following words are repeated: 'Everything else is paper,' which means that it does not produce a living impression.

"When the music is finished the second part of the ceremony begins, as is the custom at students' meetings where the dealing with serious affairs is followed by the gay part of the gathering. There are serene and mature human beings. One walks to and fro, others talk together, they welcome each other, and wine from the episcopal seminary and other drinks are served. In the form of a toast one wishes the church a favorable development and a radio amplifier plays a ragtime melody with the refrain: 'Charles is now also in the game.' It is as if the pleasure concerning some new member of the society were to be expressed by that performance. A priest explains to me: 'These somewhat futile amusements are officially acknowledged and admitted. We must adapt a little to American methods. If you have to deal with big crowds, as we have, it is inevitable. We differ however on principle from the American churches in that we cherish an emphatically anti-ascetic tendency.' Whereupon I woke up with a feeling of great relief."

There are numerous works, as you know, concerning the phenomenology of dreams, but very few that deal with their psychology. This for the obvious reason that it is a most ticklish and risky business. Freud has made a courageous effort to elucidate the intricacies of dream psychology by the aid of views which he has gathered in the field of psychopathology.[14] Much as I admire the boldness of his attempt, I cannot agree with his method and its results. He explains the dream as a mere façade, behind which something has been carefully hidden. There is no doubt that neurotics hide disagreeable things, probably just as much as normal people do. But it is a serious question whether this category can be applied to such a normal and world-wide phenomenon as the dream. I am doubtful whether we can assume that a dream is something else than it appears to be. I am rather inclined to quote another Jewish authority, the Talmud, which says: "The dream is its own interpretation." In other words I take the dream for granted. The dream is such a difficult and intricate subject, that I do not dare to make any assumptions about its possible cunning. The dream is a natural event and there is no reason under the sun why we should assume that it is a crafty device to lead us astray. The dream occurs when consciousness and will are to a great extent extinguished. It seems to be a natural product which is also to be found in people who are not neurotic. Moreover, we know so little about the psychology of the dream process that we must be more than careful when we introduce elements foreign to the dream itself into its explanation.

For all these reasons I hold that our dream really speaks of religion and that it means to do so. Since the dream is elaborate and consistent it suggests a certain logic and a certain intention, that is, it is preceded by a motivation in the unconscious which finds direct expression in the dream content.

The first part of the dream is a serious statement in favor of the Catholic church. A certain Protestant point of view—that religion is an individual experience—is discouraged by the dreamer. The second, more grotesque part, is an adaptation by the church to a decidedly worldly point of view and the end is a statement in favor of an anti-ascetic tendency which would not and could not be backed up by the real church. But the dreamer's anti-ascetic priest makes it a matter of principle. Spiritualization and sublimation are emphatically Christian principles and any insistence upon the contrary would amount to a blasphemous paganism. Christianity has never been worldly nor has it ever cherished a friendly neighborliness with good wine and food, and it is more than doubtful whether the introduction of jazz music into the cult would be a particular asset. The "serene and mature" personalities, that peripatetically converse with each other in a more or less Epicurean style, remind one much more of an antique philosophic ideal, which is rather distasteful to the contemporary Christian. In the first as well as in the second part the importance of masses or crowds is stressed.

Thus the Catholic church, though it is strongly recommended, appears to be coupled with a strange pagan point of view which is irreconcilable to a fundamentally Christian attitude. The real irreconcilability does not appear in the dream. It is hushed up as it were by a "gemütliche" atmosphere, in which dangerous contrasts are blurred and blended. The Protestant point of view of an individual relationship to God is overpowered by mass organization and correspondingly collective religious feeling. The insistence upon crowds and the insinuation of a pagan ideal are peculiar parallels to things that actually happen in Europe. Everybody wondered about paganism in modern Germany, because nobody knew how to interpret Nietzsche's Dionysian experience. Nietzsche was

but one case among thousands and millions of then
future Germans in whose unconscious the Germanic
cousin of Dionysos, that is, Wotan, developed during
the Great War.[15] In the dreams of the Germans whom
I treated then I could see clearly the Wotanistic
revolution coming on, and in 1918 I published an
article in which I pointed out the peculiar kind of
new development which was to be expected in Germany.[16] Those Germans were by no means people who
had studied *Thus Spake Zarathustra,* and surely
those young people who started the pagan sacrifices
of sheep did not know of Nietzsche's experience.[17]
Therefore they called their god Wotan and not
Dionysos. In Nietzsche's biography you will find
irrefutable proofs that the god he originally meant
was really Wotan, but, being a philologist and living
in the seventies and eighties of the nineteenth century, he called him Dionysos. Looked at from a comparative standpoint, the two gods have indeed much
in common.

There is apparently no opposition to collective
feeling, mass religion and paganism in the whole
dream of my patient, except the soon-silenced Protestant friend. There is only one curious incident de-
serving our attention: that is the unknown woman
who first supports the eulogy of Catholicism and then
suddenly weeps, saying: "Then there is nothing left
at all," and vanishes without returning.

Who is this woman? She is to the dreamer a vague
and unknown person, but when he had that dream he

was already well acquainted with her as the "unknown woman" who had frequently appeared in previous dreams.

As this figure plays a great role in men's dreams, it carries the technical designation "anima,"[18] owing to the fact that since time immemorial man in his myths always manifested the idea of a coexistence of male and female in the same body. Such psychological intuitions were usually projected in the form of the divine Syzygia, the divine pair, or of the idea of the hermaphroditic nature of the creator.[19] Edward Maitland, the biographer of Anna Kingsford, relates in our own day an inner experience of the bisexual nature of the Deity,[20] then there is Hermetic philosophy with its hermaphrodite and its androgynous inner man,[21] the "homo Adamicus," who "though he appears in male form, always carries Eve, that is, his woman, with him, concealed in his body," as a medieval commentator of the *Hermetis Tractatus Aureus* says.[22]

The anima is presumably a psychical representation of the minority of female genes in a male body. This is all the more probable as the same figure is not to be found in the imagery of a feminine unconscious. There is a corresponding figure, however, that plays an equivalent role, yet it is not a woman's image but a man's. This male figure in a woman's psychology has been designated "animus."[23] One of the most typical manifestations of both figures is what has long been called "animosity." The anima causes illogical moods, and the animus produces irritating topics and unreasonable opinions. Both are frequent dream figures. As a rule they personify the unconscious and give it its peculiarly disagreeable or irritating character. The unconscious in itself has no such negative qualities. They appear only when it is personified by those figures and they begin to influence consciousness. Being only partial personalities they have the character either of an inferior woman or of an inferior man, hence their irritating influence. A man experiencing this will be subject to unaccountable moods and a woman will be argumentative and will produce opinions which are beside the mark.

The wholly negative reaction of the anima to the church dream points out that the dreamer's feminine, that is, his unconscious, side disagrees with his attitude. The disagreement originates with the sentence on the wall: "Do not flatter your benefactor," with which the dreamer agrees. The meaning of the sentence seems to be sound enough, so that one does not understand why the woman should feel so desperate about it. Without delving further into this mystery, we must content ourselves for the time being with the fact that there is a contradiction in the dream and that a very important minority has left the stage under vivid protest and gives no more attention to the further proceedings.

We gather, then, from the dream, that the unconscious functioning of the dreamer's mind produces a pretty flat compromise between Catholicism and a pagan joie de vivre. The product of the unconscious is manifestly not expressing a point of view or a definite opinion, it is rather a dramatic exposition of an act of deliberation. It could be formulated perhaps in the following way: "Now what about this religious business? You are a Catholic, are you not? Is that not good enough? But asceticism—well, well, even the church has to adapt a little—movies, radio, spiritual five o'clock tea and all that—why not some ecclesiastical wine and gay acquaintances?" But for some secret reason this awkward mystery woman, well known from many former dreams, seems to be deeply disappointed and quits.

I must confess I find myself in sympathy with the anima. Obviously the compromise is too cheap and too superficial, but characteristic of the dreamer as well as of many other people to whom religion does not matter very much. Religion was of no concern to my patient and he certainly never expected that it would concern him in any way. But he had come to me because of a very serious experience. Being highly rationalistic and intellectual he had found that his attitude of mind and his philosophy forsook him completely in the face of his neurosis and its demoralizing forces. He found nothing in his whole Weltanschauung that would help him to gain a sufficient control over himself. He therefore was very much in the situation of a man deserted by his heretofore cherished convictions and ideals. It is by no means an extraordinary case that under such conditions a man should return to the religion of his childhood in the hope of finding something helpful there. It was, however, not a conscious attempt or a decision to revivify former religious beliefs. He merely dreamed it; that is, his unconscious produced a peculiar statement about his religion. It is just as if the spirit and the flesh, the eternal enemies in Christian consciousness, had made peace with each other in the form of a curious mitigation of their contradictory nature. Spirituality and worldliness come together in unexpected peacefulness. The effect is somewhat grotesque and comical. The inexorable severity of the spirit seems to be undermined by an almost antique gaiety, perfumed by wine and roses. The dream certainly describes a spiritual and worldly atmosphere that dulls the sharpness of a moral conflict and swallows up in oblivion all mental pain and distress.

If this was a wish fulfilment, it was surely a conscious one, for it was precisely what the patient had already overdone. And he was not unconscious about this either, since wine was one of his most dangerous enemies. The dream is, on the contrary, an impartial statement of the patient's spiritual condition. It is the picture of a degenerate religion corrupted by worldliness and mob instincts. There is religious sentimentality instead of the numinosum of divine experience. This is the well-known characteristic of a religion that has lost the living mystery. It is easily understandable that such a religion is incapable of giving help or of having any other moral effect.

The general aspect of the dream is surely unfavorable although certain other aspects of a more positive nature are dimly visible. It rarely occurs that dreams are either exclusively positive or exclusively negative. As a rule one finds both aspects, but usually one is stronger than the other. It is obvious that such a dream provides the psychologist with enough material to raise the problem of a religious attitude. If our dream were the only one we possess, we could hardly hope to unlock its innermost meaning, but we have quite a number of dreams in our series which suggest a strange religious problem. I never, if I can help it, interpret one dream by itself. As a rule a dream belongs in a series. As there is a continuity in consciousness, despite the fact that it is regularly interrupted by sleep, there is probably also a continuity of unconscious processes and perhaps even more so than with the events of consciousness. In any case my experience is in favor of the probability that dreams are the visible links in a chain of unconscious events. If we want any light on the question of the deeper reasons for the dream, we must go back to the series and find out where it has its position in the long chain of the four hundred dreams.

We find our dream wedged in between two important dreams of an uncanny quality. The dream before reports that there is a gathering of many people and that a peculiar ceremony is taking place, apparently of magic character, with the purpose of "reconstructing the gibbon." The dream after is occupied with a similar theme—the magic transformation of animals into human beings.

Both dreams are intensely disagreeable and very alarming to the patient. Whereas the church dream manifestly moves on the surface and exhibits opinions which in other circumstances could as well be thought consciously, these two dreams are strange and remote in character and their emotional effect is such that the dreamer would avoid them if possible. As a matter of fact, the text of the second dream literally says: "If one runs away, everything is lost." This remark coincides curiously with that of the unknown woman: "Then there is nothing left at all." The inference we draw from these remarks is that the church dream was an attempt at escape from other dream thoughts of a much deeper significance. Those thoughts appear spuriously in the dreams occurring before and after it.

II

DOGMA AND NATURAL SYMBOLS

THE first of these dreams—the one preceding the church dream—speaks of a ceremony through which an ape is to be reconstructed. To explain this point sufficiently would require too many details. I must, therefore, restrict myself to the mere statement that the "ape" refers to the dreamer's instinctive personality which he had completely neglected in favor of an exclusively intellectual attitude. The result had been that his instincts got the better of him and attacked him at times in uncontrollable outbursts. The "reconstruction" of the ape means the rebuilding of the instinctive personality within the framework of the hierarchy of consciousness. Such a reconstruction is only possible if accompanied by important alterations of the conscious attitude. The patient was naturally afraid of the tendencies of the unconscious, because they hitherto had revealed themselves to him in their most unfavorable form. The church dream which followed represents an attempt to seek refuge from this fear in the shelter of a church religion. The third dream, in speaking of the "transformation of animals into human beings," obviously continues the theme of the first one, that is, the ape is reconstructed merely for the purpose of being transformed later into a human being. He would be a new being, in other words, the patient has to undergo an important change through the reintegration of his hitherto split-off instinctivity, and is thus to be made over into a new man. The modern mind has forgotten those old truths that speak of the death of the old man and of the making of a new one, of spiritual rebirth and similar old-fashioned "mystical absurdities." My patient, being a scientist of today, was more than once seized by panic when he realized how much he was gripped by such thoughts. He was afraid of becoming insane, whereas the man of two thousand years ago would have welcomed such dreams and rejoiced in the hope of a magical rebirth and renewal of life. But our modern attitude looks back proudly upon the mists of superstition and of medieval or primitive credulity and entirely forgets that it carries the whole living past in the lower stories of the skyscraper of rational consciousness. Without the lower stories our mind is suspended in mid-air. No wonder that it gets nervous. The true history of the mind is not preserved in learned volumes but in the living mental organism of everyone.

I must admit, however, that the idea of renewal took on shapes such as could easily shock a modern mind. It is indeed difficult, if not impossible, to connect "rebirth," as it appears to us, with the way it is depicted by the dreams.

But before we enter upon the intimations of a

strange and unexpected transformation, we should give some attention to the other manifestly religious dream to which I alluded before.

While the church dream is relatively early in the long series, the following dream belongs to the later stages of the process.

This is the literal text:

"I am entering a solemn house. It is called 'the house of inner composure or self-collection.' In the background are many burning candles arranged so as to form four pyramid-like points. An old man stands at the door of the house. People enter, they do not talk and often stand still in order to concentrate. The old man at the door tells me about the visitors to the house and says: 'When they leave they are pure.' I enter the house now, and I am able to concentrate completely. A voice says: 'What thou art doing is dangerous. Religion is not a tax which thou payest in order to get rid of the woman's image, for this image is indispensable. Woe to those who use religion as a substitute for the other side of the soul's life. They are in error and they shall be cursed. Religion is no substitute, but it is the ultimate accomplishment added to every other activity of the soul. Out of the fulness of life thou shalt give birth to thy religion, only then shalt thou be blessed.' Together with the last sentence a faint music becomes audible, simple tunes played by an organ, reminding me somewhat of Wagner's 'fire magic' (Feuerzauber). As I leave the house I have the vision of a flaming mountain and I feel that a fire which cannot be quenched must be a sacred fire."

The patient is deeply impressed by the dream. It is a solemn and far-reaching experience to him, one of several which produced a complete change in his attitude to life and humanity.

It is not difficult to see that this dream is a parallel to the church dream. Only this time the church has become a "house of solemnity" and "self-collection." There are no indications of ceremonies or of any other known attributes of a Catholic church, with the sole exception of the burning candles, which are arranged in a symbolic form probably derived from the Catholic cult.[1] They form four pyramids or points, which perhaps anticipate the final vision of the flaming mountain in a fourfold aspect. The appearance of the number four is, however, a regular occurrence in his dreams and plays a most important role. The sacred fire mentioned refers to Bernard Shaw's *Saint Joan*, as the dreamer himself observes. The "unquenchable" fire, on the other hand, is a well-known attribute of the Deity, not only in the Old Testament, but also as an allegoria Christi in a non-canonical logion, mentioned in the Homilies of Origenes:[2] "Ait ipse salvator: qui iuxta me est, iuxta ignem est, qui longe est a me, longe est a regno." Whoever is near to me, is near to the fire; whoever is far from me, is far from the kingdom. Since Heraclitus, life has been figured as a πῦρ ἀείζωον, an eternally living fire, and as Christ designates himself as

The Life, the noncanonical saying is understandable, even credible. The fire symbolism with the meaning of "life" fits into the frame of the dream, for it emphasizes the "fulness of life" as being the only legitimate source of religion. Thus the four fiery points function almost as an icon denoting the presence of the Deity or of an equivalent idea. As I said before, the number four plays an important part in these dreams, always alluding to an idea akin to the Pythagorean τετρακτύς.[3]

The quaternarium or quaternity has a long history. It not only appears in Christian iconology and mystical speculation,[4] but it plays a perhaps still greater role in Gnostic philosophy[5] and from thereon down through the Middle Ages as far as the eighteenth century.[6]

In the dream under discussion the quaternity appears as the most significant exponent of the religious cult created by the unconscious mind. The dreamer enters the "house of self-collection" alone, instead of with a friend as in the church dream. Here he meets an old man, who had already appeared in a former dream as the sage and who had designated a particular spot on the earth where the dreamer belonged. The old man explains the character of the cult to be a purification ritual. It is not clear, however, from the dream text what kind of purification is referred to, or from what it should purify. The only ritual that actually takes place seems to be a concentration or meditation, leading to the ecstatic phenomenon of the voice. The voice is a frequent occurrence in this dream series. It always pronounces an authoritative declaration or command, either of astonishing common sense and truth, or of profound philosophic allusion. It is nearly always a definite statement, usually coming toward the end of a dream, and it is, as a rule, so clear and convincing that the dreamer finds no argument against it. It has, indeed, so much the character of indisputable truth that it often appears as the final and absolutely valid summing up of a long unconscious deliberation and weighing of arguments. Frequently the voice issues from an authoritative figure, as from a military commander, or the captain of a ship, or an old physician. Sometimes, as for instance in this case, there is simply a voice coming apparently from nowhere. It was of considerable interest to see how this very intellectual and skeptical man accepted the voice; often it did not suit him at all, yet he accepted it unquestioningly, and even humbly. Thus the voice revealed itself during the course of many hundred carefully recorded dreams as an important and even decisive representation of the unconscious. In as much as this patient is by no means the only case under my observation that has exhibited the phenomenon of the voice in dreams and in other peculiar conditions of consciousness, I have to admit the fact that the unconscious mind is capable at times of assuming an intelligence and purposiveness which are superior to actual conscious insight. There is hardly any doubt that this fact is a basic religious phenomenon, which is observed here in a case whose conscious mental make-up was certainly most unlikely to produce religious phenomena. I have not infrequently made similar observations in other cases and I must confess that I am unable to formulate the data in any other way. I have often met with the objection that the thoughts which the voice represents are no more than the thoughts of the individual himself. That may be; but I would call a thought my own when *I* have thought it, as I would call money my own when I have earned or acquired it in a conscious and legitimate way. If somebody gives me the money as a present, then I will certainly not say to my benefactor, "Thank you for my own money," although to a third person and afterward I might say: "This is my own money." With the voice I am in a similar situation. The voice gives me certain contents, exactly as a friend would inform me of his ideas. It would be neither decent nor true to suggest that what he says are my own ideas.

This is the reason why I differentiate between that which I have produced or acquired by my own conscious effort and that which is clearly and unmistakably a product of the unconscious mind. Someone may object that the so-called unconscious mind is merely my own mind and that, therefore, such a differentiation is superfluous. But I am not at all certain whether the unconscious mind is merely *my* mind, because the term "unconscious" means that I

am not even conscious of it. As a matter of fact the
concept of the unconscious mind is a mere assumption
for the sake of convenience.[7] In reality I am totally
unconscious of—in other words, I do not know at all
—where the voice originates. I am not only incapable
of producing the phenomenon at will but I am also
unable to anticipate the mental contents of the voice.
Under such conditions it would be presumptuous to
call the factor which produces the voice *my* mind.
This would not be accurate. The fact that you perceive the voice in your dream proves nothing at all,
for you can also hear the noises in the street, which
you would not explain as your own.

There is only one condition under which you might
legitimately call the voice your own, namely, when
you assume your conscious personality to be a part
of a whole or to be a smaller circle contained in a big-
ger one. A little bank clerk, showing a friend around
town, who points out the bank building, saying, "And
here is *my* bank," is using the same privilege.

We may assume that human personality consists of
two things: first, of consciousness and whatever this
covers, and second, of an indefinitely large hinterland
of unconscious psyche. So far as the former is concerned it can be more or less clearly defined and delimited, but so far as the sum total of human personality is concerned one has to admit the impossibility
of a complete description or definition. In other
words, there is unavoidably an illimitable and indefinable addition to every personality, because the lat-

ter consists of a conscious and observable part which does not contain certain factors whose existence, however, we are forced to assume in order to explain certain observable facts. The unknown factors form what we call the unconscious.

Of what those factors consist, we have no idea, since we can observe only their effects. We may assume that they are of a psychical nature comparable to that of conscious contents, yet there is no certainty about this. But if we imagine such a likeness we can hardly refrain from going further. Since the contents of our minds are only conscious and perceivable in so far as they are associated with an ego, the phenomenon of the voice, having a strongly personal character, may also issue from a center—one, however, which is not identical with that of our conscious ego. Such reasoning is permissible if we conceive of the ego as being subordinated to, or contained in, a superordinated self as a center of the total, illimitable and indefinable psychic personality.[8]

I do not enjoy philosophical arguments that amuse through their own complications. Although my argument seems to be abstruse, it is at least an honest attempt to formulate observed facts. To put it simply one could say: Since we do not know everything, practically each experience, fact or object contains something which is unknown. Hence if we speak of the totality of an experience, the word "totality" can refer only to the conscious part of the experience. As we cannot assume that our experience covers the totality of the object, it is evident, that its absolute totality must needs contain the part that has not been experienced. The same holds true, as I have mentioned, of every experience and also of the psyche, whose absolute totality covers a greater surface than consciousness. In other words, the psyche is no exception to the general rule that the universe can be established only in as far as our psychic organism permits.

My psychological experience has shown time and again that certain contents issue from a psyche more complete than consciousness. They often contain a superior analysis or insight or knowledge which consciousness has not been able to produce. We have a suitable word for such occurrences—intuition. In pronouncing it, most people have an agreeable feeling as if something had been settled. But they never take into account the fact that you do not *make* an intuition. On the contrary it always comes to you; you *have* a hunch, it has produced itself and you only catch it if you are clever or quick enough.

Consequently I explain the voice, in the dream of the sacred house, as a product of the more complete personality to which the dreamer's conscious self belongs as a part, and I hold that this is the reason why the voice shows an intelligence and a clarity superior to the dreamer's actual consciousness. This superiority is the reason for the unconditioned authority of the voice.

The message of the voice contains a strange criticism of the dreamer's attitude. In the church dream he has made an attempt to reconcile two sides of life by a kind of cheap compromise. As we know, the unknown woman, the anima, disagreed and left the scene. In the present dream the voice seems to have taken the place of the anima, making not a merely emotional protest but rather a masterful statement about two kinds of religion. According to this statement, the dreamer is inclined to use religion as a substitute for the "image of the woman," as the text says. The "woman" refers to the anima. This is borne out by the next sentence, which speaks of religion being used as a substitute for "the other side of the soul's life." The anima is the "other side," as I explained before. She is the representative of the female minority concealed below the threshold of consciousness, that is to say, the so-called unconscious mind. The critique, therefore, would read as follows: "You try religion in order to escape from your unconscious. You use it as a substitute for a part of your soul's life. But religion is the fruit and the culmination of the completeness of life, that is, of a life which contains both sides."

A careful comparison with other dreams of the same series shows unmistakably what the "other side" is. The patient always tried to avoid his emotional needs. As a matter of fact he was afraid that they might get him into trouble, into marriage, for instance, and into other responsibilities such as love, devotion, loyalty, confidence, emotional dependence and general submission to the soul's needs. All this had nothing to do with science or an academic career; and, moreover, the word "soul" was nothing but an intellectual obscenity, not to be touched with a barge pole.

The "mystery" of the anima is the religious innuendo, a great puzzle to my patient, who naturally enough knew nothing of religion except that it was a creed. And he understood that religion can be a substitute for certain awkward emotional demands which one might circumvent by going to church. The prejudices of our age are visibly reflected in the dreamer's apprehensions. The voice, on the other hand, is unorthodox, it is even unconventional to a shocking degree: it takes religion seriously, puts it upon the very apex of life, of a life containing "either side," and thus upsets the most cherished intellectual and rationalistic prejudices. This was such an overturn that my patient was often afraid he might go crazy. Well, I should say that we—knowing the average intellectual of today or of yesterday—can easily sympathize with his predicament. To take the "image of the woman"—in other words, the unconscious mind—into account earnestly, what a blow to enlightened common sense![9]

I began his personal treatment only after he had observed the first series of about three hundred and fifty dreams. Then I got the whole backwash of his upsetting experience. No wonder that he wanted to run away from his adventure! But fortunately enough the man had "religion," that is, he "carefully took into account" his experience and he had πίστις enough, or loyalty to his experience, to enable him to cling to it and to continue it. He had the great advantage of being neurotic and so, whenever he tried to be disloyal to his experience or to deny the voice, the neurotic condition instantly came back. He simply could not "quench the fire" and finally he had to admit the incomprehensibly numinous character of his experience. He had to confess that the unquenchable fire was "sacred." This was the conditio sine qua non of his cure.

One might, perhaps, consider this case an exception in as much as really human and complete persons are exceptions. It is true that an overwhelming majority of educated people are fragmentary personalities and have a lot of substitutes instead of the genuine goods. Being like that meant a neurosis for this man, and it means the same for a great many other people.

What is usually and generally called "religion" is to such an amazing degree a substitute that I ask myself seriously whether this kind of "religion," which I prefer to call a creed, has not an important function in human society. The substitution has the obvious purpose of replacing immediate experience by a choice of suitable symbols invested in a solidly organized dogma and ritual. The Catholic church maintains them by her indisputable authority, the Protestant church (if this term is still applicable) by insistence upon faith and the evangelical message. As long as those two principles work, people are effectively defended and shielded against immediate religious experience.[10] Even if something of the sort should happen to them, they can refer to the church, for it would know whether the experience came from God or from the devil, whether it was to be accepted or to be rejected.

In my profession I have encountered many cases of people who have had such an immediate experience, and who would not submit to the authority of dogmatic decision. I had to accompany them through the peripeties of passionate conflicts, panics of madness, desperate confusions and depressions which were grotesque and terrible at the same time, so that I am amply aware of the extraordinary importance of dogma and ritual, at least as methods of mental hygiene. If the patient is a practicing Catholic, I invariably advise him to confess and to communicate in order to protect himself from immediate experience, which might easily be too much for him. With Protestants it is usually not so easy, because dogma and ritual have become so pale and faint that they have lost their efficacy to a high degree. There is also, as a rule, no confession and the parsons share in the common dislike of psychological problems and also, unfortunately, in the common psychological ignorance. The Catholic "director of conscience" has often infinitely more psychological skill and insight. Protestant parsons, moreover, have undergone a scientific training at a theological faculty which, owing to its

critical spirit, undermines naïveté of faith, whereas
the overwhelming historical tradition in a Catholic
priest's training is apt to strengthen the authority
of the institution.

As a doctor I might, of course, adhere to the so-
called "scientific" creed, holding that the contents of
a neurosis are nothing but repressed infantile sexuality or will to power and, by thus depreciating these
contents, it would be possible to a certain extent to
shield a number of patients from the risk of immediate experience. But I know that this theory is only
partially true, which means that it formulates only
certain superficial aspects of the neurotic psyche.
And I cannot tell my patients what I myself do not
fully believe.

Now people may ask me: "But if you tell your
practicing Catholic to go to the priest and confess,
you are also telling him something which you do not
believe"—that is, assuming that I am a Protestant.

In order to answer this critical question I must declare first that, if I can help it, I never preach my belief. If asked I shall surely stand by my convictions
which do not go further than what I consider to be
my actual knowledge. I am convinced of what I *know*.
Everything else is hypothesis and beyond that I can
leave a lot of things to the Unknown. They do not
bother me. But they would begin to bother me, I am
sure, if I felt that I *ought* to know something about
them.

If, therefore, a patient should be convinced of the

exclusively sexual origin of his neurosis, I would not
disturb him in his opinion because I know that such
a conviction, particularly if it is deeply rooted, is an
excellent defense against an onslaught of the terrible
ambiguity of an immediate experience. As long as
such a defense works I shall not break it down, since
I know that there must be powerful reasons why the
patient has to think in such a narrow circle. But if his
dreams should begin to destroy the protective theory,
I have to support the wider personality, as I have
done in the dream case described.

In the same way and for the same reason, I support the hypothesis of the practicing Catholic while
it works for him. In either case I support a means of
defense against a grave risk, without asking the academic question whether the defense is more or less an
ultimate truth. I am glad when and as long as it
works.

With our patient the Catholic defense had broken
down long before I even touched the case. He would
have laughed at me if I had advised him to confess or
anything of the sort, as he laughed at the sex theory,
which was not one to be supported with him either.
But I always let him see that I was entirely on the
side of the voice, which I recognized as part of his
future greater personality, destined to relieve him of
his onesidedness.

To a certain intellectual mediocrity, characterized
by enlightened rationalism, a scientific theory that
simplifies matters is a very good means of defense, be-

cause of the tremendous faith of modern man in anything which bears the label "scientific." Such a label
sets your mind at rest immediately, almost as well as
"Roma locuta causa finita." In itself any scientific
theory, no matter how subtle, has, I think, less value
from the standpoint of psychological truth than the
religious dogma, for the simple reason that a theory
is necessarily highly abstract and exclusively rational,
whereas the dogma expresses an irrational entity
through the image. This method guarantees a much
better rendering of an irrational fact, such as the
psyche. Moreover, the dogma owes its existence and
form, on the one hand, to so-called "revealed" immediate experiences, such as the God-Man, the Cross,
the Virgin Birth, the Immaculate Conception, the
Trinity and so on, and, on the other hand, to the
ceaseless collaboration of many minds and many centuries. It is perhaps not quite clear why I call certain
dogmas "immediate experiences," since a dogma is
in itself the very thing which excludes immediate experience. Yet the Christian dogmas which I mentioned
are not peculiar to Christianity alone. They occur
just as often in pagan religions and, moreover, they
can reappear spontaneously as psychical phenomena
in all kinds of variations, as they have, in a remote
past, originated from visions, dreams, or trances.
Such ideas were never invented. They came into existence when mankind had not yet learned to use the
mind as a purposeful activity. Before people learned
to produce thoughts the thought came to them. They

did not think but perceived their mental function.
The dogma is like a dream, reflecting the spontaneous
and autonomous activity of the objective psyche, the
unconscious. Such an expression of the unconscious is
a much more efficient means of defense against further immediate experiences than a scientific theory.
The theory has to disregard the emotional values of
the experience. The dogma, on the contrary, is most
expressive in this respect. A scientific theory is soon
superseded by another. The dogma lasts for untold
centuries. The suffering God-Man may be at least
five thousand years old and the Trinity is probably
even older.

The dogma represents the soul more completely
than a scientific theory, for the latter expresses and
formulates the conscious mind alone. Furthermore, a
theory can do nothing but formulate a living thing
by abstract notions. The dogma, on the contrary, expresses aptly the living process of the unconscious in
the form of the drama of repentance, sacrifice and redemption. It is rather astonishing, from this point of
view, that the Protestant schism could not have been
avoided. But since Protestantism has become the creed
of the adventurous Germanic tribes with their characteristic curiosity, acquisitiveness and recklessness,
it seems to be possible that their peculiar character
could not quite agree with the peace of the church, at
least not for any length of time. It looks as if they
were not quite prepared to have a process of salvation happen to them and for a submission to a deity

crystallized in the magnificent structure of the church. There was, perhaps, too much of the Imperium Romanum or of the Pax Romana in the church, too much, at least, for their energies that were and are still insufficiently domesticated. It is quite likely that they were in need of an unmitigated and less controlled experience of God, as often happens to adventurous and restless people, too youthful for any form of conservatism or resignation. They removed therefore the intercession of the church between God and man, some more and some less. Owing to the abolition of protective walls the Protestant has lost the sacred images expressive of important unconscious factors, together with the ritual, which, since time immemorial, has been a safe way of dealing with the unaccountable forces of the unconscious mind. A great amount of energy thus became liberated and went instantly into the old channels of curiosity and acquisitiveness, by which Europe became the mother of dragons that devoured the greater part of the earth.

Since those days Protestantism has become a hotbed of schisms and, at the same time, of a rapid increase of science and technics which attracted human consciousness to such an extent that it forgot the unaccountable forces of the unconscious mind. The catastrophe of the Great War and the subsequent extraordinary manifestations of a profound mental disturbance were needed to arouse a doubt that everything was well with the white man's mind. When the war broke out we had been quite certain that the world could be righted by rational means. Now we behold the amazing spectacle of States taking over the age-old claim of theocracy, that is, of totality, inevitably accompanied by suppression of free opinion. We again see people cutting each other's throats to support childish theories of how to produce paradise on earth. It is not very difficult to see that the powers of the underworld—not to say of hell—which were formerly more or less successfully chained and made serviceable in a gigantic mental edifice, are now creating, or trying to create, a State slavery and a State prison devoid of any mental or spiritual charm. There are not a few people, nowadays, who are convinced that mere human reason is not entirely up to the enormous task of fettering the volcano.

This whole development is fate. I would not blame Protestantism or the Renaissance for it. But one thing is certain—that modern man, Protestant or not, has lost the protection of the ecclesiastical walls carefully erected and reinforced since Roman days, and on account of that loss has approached the zone of world-destroying and world-creating fire. Life has become quickened and intensified. Our world is permeated by waves of restlessness and fear.

Protestantism was, and still is, a great risk and at the same time a great opportunity. If it keeps on disintegrating as a church, it succeeds in depriving man of all his spiritual safeguards and means of defense against the immediate experience of the forces waiting for liberation in the unconscious mind. Look at all the incredible savagery going on in our so-called civilized world, all of which is derived from human beings and their mental condition! Look at the devilish means of destruction! They are invented by perfectly harmless gentlemen, reasonable, respectable citizens, being all we hope to be. And when the whole thing blows up and causes an indescribable inferno of devastation, nobody seems to be responsible. It simply occurs, yet it is all man made. But since every person is blindly convinced that he is nothing but his very modest and unimportant consciousness, which neatly fulfils duties and earns a moderate living, nobody is aware that this whole rationally organized crowd, called a state or a nation, is run by a seemingly impersonal, imperceptible but terrific power, checked by nobody and by nothing. This ghastly power is mostly explained by fear of the neighboring nation, which is supposed to be possessed by a malevolent devil. As nobody is capable of recognizing where and how much he himself is possessed and unconscious, one simply projects one's own condition upon the neighbor, and thus it becomes a sacred duty to have the biggest guns and the most poisonous gas. The worst of it is that one is quite right. All one's neighbors are ruled by an uncontrolled and uncontrollable fear just like oneself. In lunatic asylums it is a well-known fact that patients are far more dangerous when suffering from fear than when moved by wrath or hatred.

The Protestant is left to God alone. There is no
confession, no absolution, no possibility of any kind
of an atoning opus divinum. He has to digest his sins
alone and he is not too sure of divine grace, which has
become unattainable through lack of a suitable ritual.
Owing to this fact the Protestant conscience has become wakeful, and this bad conscience has acquired a
disagreeable tendency to linger and to make people
uncomfortable. But through this the Protestant has
a unique chance to realize sin to a degree hardly at-
tainable by Catholic mentality, for confession and
absolution are always ready to relieve too much tension. But the Protestant is left to his tension, which
can continue to sharpen his conscience. Conscience,
and particularly bad conscience, can be a gift from
heaven; a genuine grace, if used as a superior self-
criticism. Self-criticism, as an introspective, discriminating activity, is indispensable to any attempt to
understand one's own psychology. If you have done
something which puzzles you and you ask yourself
what has prompted you to such an action, you need
the motive of a bad conscience and its corresponding
discriminating faculty in order to discover the real
motive of your behavior. It is only then that you are
able to see what motives are ruling your deeds. The
sting of bad conscience even spurs you on to discover
things which were unconscious before and in this way
you might cross the threshold of the unconscious
mind and become aware of those impersonal forces
that make you the unconscious instrument of the

wholesale murderer in man. If a Protestant survives
the complete loss of his church and still remains a
Protestant, that is, a man who is defenseless against
God and is no longer shielded by walls or by com-
munities, he has the unique spiritual chance of immediate religious experience.

I do not know whether I have succeeded in convey-
ing what the experience of the unconscious mind
meant to my patient. There is, however, no objective
measure for the value of such experience. We have to
take it for what it is worth to the person who has the
experience. Thus you may be impressed by the fact
that the apparent futility of certain dreams should
mean something to an intelligent person. But if you
cannot accept what he says, or if you cannot put
yourself in his place, you should not judge his case.
The genius religiosus is a wind that bloweth where it
listeth. There is no Archimedean point from which to
judge, since the psyche is indistinguishable from its
manifestation. The psyche is the object of psychology, and—fatally enough—its subject at the
same time and there is no getting away from this
fact.

The few dreams I have chosen as an example of
what I call "immediate experience" are surely unob-
trusive to the inexperienced eye. They make no show,
being modest witnesses of a merely individual experience. They would cut a better figure if I could
present them in their sequence, together with that
wealth of symbolic material which was brought up in

the course of the whole process. But even the sum total of the series of dreams could not compare in beauty and expressiveness to any part of a traditional creed. A creed is always the result and fruit of many minds and many centuries, purified from all the oddities, shortcomings and flaws of individual experience. But for all that, the individual experience, with its very poverty, is immediate life, it is the warm red blood pulsating today. It is more convincing to a seeker after truth than the best tradition. Yet immediate life is always individual, since the carrier of life is the individual, and whatever emanates from the individual is in a way unique, transitory and imperfect; particularly so when it is a matter of involuntary mental products such as dreams and the like. No one else will have the same dreams, although many have the same problem. But just as there is no individual differentiated to a condition of absolute uniqueness, so also there are no individual products of an absolutely unique quality. Even dreams are made of collective material to a very high degree, just as, in the mythology and folklore of different peoples, certain motives repeat themselves in almost identical form. I have called those motives archetypes[11] and by them I understand forms or images of a collective nature which occur practically all over the earth as constituents of myths and at the same time as autochthonous, individual products of unconscious origin. The archetypal motives presumably start from the archetypal patterns of the human mind which are not only transmitted by tradition and migration but also by heredity. The latter hypothesis is indispensable, since even complicated archetypal images can be spontaneously reproduced without any possible direct tradition.

The theory of preconscious, primordial ideas is by no means my own invention, as the term "archetype," which belongs to the first centuries of our era, denotes.[12] With special reference to psychology we find this theory in the works of Adolf Bastian[13] and then again in Nietzsche.[14] In French literature Hubert, Mauss[15] and Lévy-Bruhl[16] mention similar ideas. I gave only an empirical foundation to the theory of what were called formerly primordial or elementary ideas, "catégories" or "habitudes directrices de la conscience," "représentations collectives," etc., by undertaking certain researches into detail.[17]

In the second of the dreams we discussed before, we met with an archetype that I have not yet taken into consideration. This is the peculiar arrangement of burning candles in four pyramid-like points. The arrangement emphasizes the symbolic importance of the number four, by putting it in place of the altar or the iconostasis, where one would expect to find the sacred images. Since the Temple is called the "house of self-collection," we may assume that this character is expressed by the image or symbol appearing in the place of worship. The tetraktys—to use the Pythagorean term—does indeed refer to "self-collection," as our patient's dream clearly demonstrates. The sym-

bol appears in other dreams, usually in the form of a
circle divided by or containing four main parts. In
other dreams of the same series it takes also the form
of an undivided circle, a flower, a square place or
room, a quadrangle, a globe, a clock, a symmetrical
garden with a fountain in the center, four people in
a boat, in an aeroplane or at a table, four chairs
round a table, four colors, a wheel with eight spokes,
an eight-rayed star or sun, a round hat divided into
eight parts, a bear with four eyes, a square prison
cell, the four seasons, a bowl containing four nuts,
the world clock with a disk divided into $4 \times 8 = 32$
divisions, and so on.[18]

Those quaternity symbols occur not less than sev-
enty-one times in a series of four hundred dreams.
My case is no exception in this respect. I have observed many cases where the four occurred and it
always had an unconscious origin, that is, the dreamer
got it first from a dream and had no idea of its meaning nor had he ever heard of the symbolic importance
of the four. It would of course be a different thing
with the three, since the Trinity represents an acknowledged symbolic number accessible to everybody.
But four with us, and particularly with a modern
scientist, conveys no more than any other number.
Number symbolism and its venerable history is a field
of knowledge utterly beyond the interests of our
dreamer's mind. If dreams, under such conditions, insist upon the importance of the four, we have every
right to call its origin an unconscious one. The numi-

nous character of the quaternity is obvious in the
second dream. From this fact we must conclude that
it points to a meaning which we have to call "sacred."
Since the dreamer is unable to trace this peculiar
character to any conscious source, I apply a comparative method in order to elucidate the meaning of
the symbolism. It is of course impossible to give a
complete account of this comparative procedure
within the frame of this book. I must, therefore, restrict myself to mere allusions.

Since many of the unconscious contents seem to be
remnants of historical mental conditions, we need only
go back a few hundred years in order to reach that
conscious level which forms the parallel to our unconscious contents. In our case we step back not quite
three hundred years and find ourselves among scientists and philosophers of nature who are seriously
discussing the enigma of the quadratura circuli.[19]
This abstruse problem was in itself a psychological
projection of much older and completely unconscious
things. But they knew in those days that the circle
meant the Deity: "Deus est figura intellectualis, cujus
centrum est ubique, circumferentia vero nusquam,"
as one of these philosophers said, repeating St. Augustine. A man as introverted and introspective as
Emerson could hardly fail to touch upon the same
idea and likewise quote St. Augustine. The image of
the circle—regarded as the most perfect form since
Plato's *Timaeus*, the prime authority of Hermetic
philosophy—was also given to the most perfect sub-

stance, to the gold, to the anima mundi or anima
media natura, and to the first created light. And because the macrocosm, the Great World, was made by
the creator "in forma rotunda et globosa,"[20] the
smallest part of the whole, the point, also contains
this perfect nature. As the philosopher says: "Omnium figurarum simplicissima et perfectissima primo
est rotunda, quae in puncto requiescit."[21] This image
of the Deity, dormant and concealed in matter, was
what the alchemists called the original chaos, or the
earth of paradise, or the round fish in the sea,[22] or
merely the rotundum or the egg. That round thing
was in possession of the key which unlocked the closed
doors of matter. As it is said in *Timaeus*, only the
demiurge, the perfect being, was capable of dissolv-
ing the tetraktys,[23] the embrace of the four elements,
that is, the four constituents of the round world. One
of the great authorities since the thirteenth century,
the *Turba Philosophorum*, says that the rotundum can
dissolve copper into four.[24] Thus the much-sought-
for aurum philosophicum was round.[25] Opinions were
divided as to the procedure by which one could pro-
cure the dormant demiurge. Some hoped to lay hold
of him in the form of a prima materia containing a
particular concentration or a specially apt kind of
substance. Others made efforts to create the round
substance by a sort of synthesis, called "conjunctio";
the Anonymus of the "Rosarium Philosophorum"
says: "Make a round circle of man and woman, extract therefrom a quadrangle and from it a triangle.

Make the circle round and thou shalt have the Philosopher's Stone."[26]

This marvelous stone was symbolized as a perfect living being of hermaphroditic nature corresponding to the Empedoclean σφαῖρος, the εὐδαιμονέστατος θεός and the all-round bisexual man of Plato.[27] As early as the beginning of the fourteenth century, the lapis was compared by Petrus Bonus to Christ as representing an allegoria Christi.[28] But in the *Aurea Hora*, a Pseudo-Thomasian tract of the thirteenth century, the mystery of the stone is paramount to the mysteries of the Christian religion.[29] I mention these facts merely to show that the circle or globe containing the four meant the Deity to not a few of our learned forefathers.

From the Latin tracts it is also evident that the latent demiurge, dormant and concealed in matter, is identical with the so-called homo philosophicus, the second Adam.[30] The latter is the superior, spiritual man, the Adam Kadmon, often identified with Christ. While the original Adam was mortal, because he consisted of the corruptible four elements, the second Adam is immortal, because he consists of one pure and incorruptible essence. Thus Pseudo-Thomas says: "Secundus Adam de puris elementis in aeternitatem transivit. Ideo quia ex simplici et pura essentia constat, in aeternum manet."[31] An early Latinized Arabic author called Senior, a famous authority throughout the Middle Ages, is quoted as saying about the lapis: "There is one substance which never dies, because it perseveres in constant increase." This substance is the second Adam.[32]

It is evident from these quotations that the round substance searched for by the philosophers was a projection of a nature very similar to our dream symbolism. We have historical documents which prove that often dreams, visions, even hallucinations, were mixed with the great philosophic opus.[33] Our forefathers, being of a more naïve mental constitution, projected their unconscious contents directly into matter. Matter, however, could easily accept such projections, because at that time it was a practically unknown and incomprehensible entity. And whenever man encounters something totally mysterious he projects his assumptions into it without the slightest self-criticism. But since chemical matter nowadays is something we know fairly well, we can no longer project as freely as our ancestors were able to do. We have, at last, to admit that the tetraktys is something psychical; and we do not know yet whether, in a more or less remote future, this may not also be proved to be a projection. For the time being we are satisfied with the fact that an idea of God, utterly absent from the conscious mind of modern man, returns in a form known consciously three hundred or four hundred years ago.

I do not need to emphasize the fact that this piece of history was completely unknown to my dreamer. One could say, quoting a classical poet:

"Naturam expellas furca tamen usque recurret."

The idea of those old philosophers was that God manifested himself first in the creation of the four elements. They were symbolized by the four partitions of the circle. Thus we read in a Coptic Gnostic tract of the *Codex Brucianus*[34] about the Only-Begotten (Monogenes or Anthropos): "This same is he who dwelleth in the Monad, which is in the Setheus (creator), and which came from the place of which none can say where it is. . . . From him it is the Monad came, in the manner of a ship, laden with all good things, and in the manner of a field, filled or planted with every kind of tree, and in the manner of a city, filled with all races of mankind . . . to its veil which surroundeth it in the manner of a defense, there are twelve Gates . . . this same is the Mother-City (μητρόπολις) of the Only-Begotten." In another place the Anthropos himself is the city and his members are the four gates. The Monad is but a spark of light (σπινθήρ), an atom of the Deity. The Monogenes is thought of as standing upon a τετράπεζα, a platform supported by four pillars corresponding to the Christian quaternarium of the Evangiles, or to the Tetramorphus, the symbolic riding animal of the church, consisting of the symbols of the four evangelists, the angel, eagle, ox or calf, and lion. The analogy of this text with the New Jerusalem of the Revelations is obvious.

The division into four, the synthesis of the four, the miraculous apparition of the four colors and the four stages of the work: the nigredo, the dealbatio, rubefactio and citrinitas, are constant preoccupations of the old philosophers.[85] The four symbolizes the parts, qualities and aspects of the One. But why should my patient repeat those old speculations?

I do not know why he should. I know only that this is not an isolated case; many other cases under my observation or under that of my colleagues have spontaneously produced the same symbolism. I do not really think that they get it from three hundred or four hundred years ago. That age was rather another time when this same archetypal idea was very much in the foreground. As a matter of fact, it is much older than the Middle Ages, as *Timaeus* proves. Nor is it a classical or an Egyptian inheritance, since it is to be found practically everywhere and in all ages. One has only to remember, for instance, how great an importance is attributed to the quaternity by the red Indians.

Although the four is an age-old, presumably prehistoric symbol,[86] always associated with the idea of a world-creating deity, it is, however—curiously enough—rarely understood as such by those modern people to whom it occurs. I have always been particularly interested to see how people, if left to their own devices and not informed about the history of the symbol, would interpret it to themselves. I was careful, therefore, not to disturb them with my own opinions and as a rule I discovered that people took it to symbolize themselves or rather something in themselves. They felt it as belonging intimately to them-

selves as a sort of creative background, a life-produc-
ing sun in the depths of the unconscious mind.
Though it was easy to see that it was often almost a
replica of Ezekiel's vision, it was very rare that people recognized the analogy, even when they knew the
vision—which knowledge, by the way, is pretty rare
nowadays. What one could almost call a systematic
blindness is simply the effect of the prejudice that
the deity is *outside* man. Although this prejudice is
not solely Christian, there are certain religions which
do not share it at all. On the contrary they insist, as
do certain Christian mystics, upon the essential identity of God and man, either in the form of an a priori
identity, or of a goal to be attained by certain practices or initiations, as we know them, for instance,
from the metamorphoses of Apuleius, not to speak of
certain yoga methods.

The application of the comparative method indubitably shows the quaternity as being a more or
less direct representation of the God manifested in his
creation. We might, therefore, conclude that the symbol, spontaneously produced in the dreams of modern
people, means the same thing—*the God within*. Although the majority of cases do not recognize this
analogy, the interpretation might nevertheless be
true. If we take into consideration the fact that the
idea of God is an "unscientific" hypothesis, we can
easily explain why people have forgotten to think
along such lines. And even if they cherish a certain
belief in God they would be deterred from the idea of

God within by their religious education, which always depreciated this idea as "mystical." Yet it is precisely this "mystical" idea which is enforced by the natural tendencies of the unconscious mind. I myself, as well as my colleagues, have seen so many cases developing the same kind of symbolism that we cannot doubt its existence any longer. My observations, moreover, date back as far as 1914 and I waited fourteen years before I alluded publicly to them.

It would be a regrettable mistake if anybody should understand my observations to be a kind of proof of the existence of God. They prove only the existence of an archetypal image of the Deity, which to my mind is the most we can assert psychologically about God. But as it is a very important and influential archetype, its relatively frequent occurrence seems to be a noteworthy fact for any theologia naturalis. Since the experience of it has the quality of numinosity, often to a high degree, it ranks among religious experiences.

I cannot omit calling attention to the interesting fact that whereas the central Christian symbolism is a Trinity, the formula of the unconscious mind is a quaternity. As a matter of fact even the orthodox Christian formula is not quite complete, because the dogmatic aspect of the evil principle is absent from the Trinity, the former leading a more or less awkward existence as devil. Since a God identical with man is a heretical assumption,[37] the "God within" is also dogmatically difficult. But the quaternity as un-

derstood by the modern mind directly suggests not
only the God within, but also the identity of God and
man. Contrary to the dogma there are not three, but
four aspects. It could easily be inferred that the
fourth represents the devil. Though we have the
logion: "I myself and the Father are one. Who seeth
me seeth the Father," it would be considered as blas-
phemy or as madness to stress Christ's dogmatic
humanity to such a degree that man could identify
himself with Christ and his homoousia. But this is
precisely the inference. From an orthodox standpoint,
therefore, the natural quaternity could be declared to
be "diabolica fraus" and the capital piece of evidence
would be the assimilation of the fourth aspect which
represents the reprehensible part of the Christian
cosmos. The church, I assume, has to invalidate any
attempt at taking such results seriously. She must
even condemn any approach to these experiences,
since she cannot admit that nature unites what she
has separated. The voice of nature is clearly audible
in all the events that are connected with the quaternity, and this arouses all the old suspicions against
anything connected with the unconscious mind. Scientific exploration of dreams is old oneiromancy and
as objectionable as alchemy. Close parallels to the
psychology of dreams are to be found among Latin
alchemical tracts and are, like these, full of heresy.[38]
There, it seems, was once reason enough for secrecy
and protective metaphors.[39] The symbolic statements
of old alchemy issue from the same unconscious mind

as modern dreams and are just as much the voice of nature.

If we were still living in a medieval setting where there was not much doubt about the ultimate things and where every history of the world began with Genesis, we could easily brush aside dreams and the like. Unfortunately we live in a modern setting, where the ultimate things are doubtful, where there is a pre-history of enormous extension, and where people are fully aware of the fact that if there is any numinous experience at all, it is the experience of the psyche. We can no longer imagine an empyrean world revolving round the throne of God, and we would not dream of seeking for Him somewhere behind the galactic systems. But the human soul seems to harbor mysteries, since to an empiricist all religious experience boils down to a peculiar condition of the mind. If we want to know anything of what religious experience means to those who have it, we have every chance nowadays of studying every imaginable form of it. And if it means anything, it means everything to those who have it. This is at least the inevitable conclusion one reaches by a careful study of the evidence. One could even define religious experience as that kind of experience which is characterized by the highest appreciation, no matter what its contents are. Modern mentality, in as much as it is formulated by the verdict "extra ecclesiam nulla salus," will turn to the soul as to a last hope. Where else could one obtain experience? The answer will be more or less of the

kind which I have described. The voice of nature will
answer and all those concerned with the spiritual
problem of man will be confronted with new baffling
problems. Through the spiritual need of my patients
I have been forced to make a serious attempt at least
to understand some of the extraordinary implications
of the symbolism produced by the unconscious mind.
As it would lead much too far to go into a discussion
of the intellectual as well as the ethical consequences,
I have to content myself with a mere allusion.

The main symbolic figures of a religion are always
expressive of the particular moral and mental attitude involved. I mention, for instance, the cross and
its various religious meanings. Another main symbol
is the Trinity. It is of an exclusively masculine character. The unconscious mind, however, transforms it
into a quaternity, being a unity at the same time,
just as the three persons of the Trinity are one and
the same God. The old philosophers of nature represented the Trinity, in as much as it was "imaginata in
natura," as the three ἀσώμαῖα or "spiritus," or "vola-
tilia," viz., water, air and fire. The fourth constituent
on the other hand was τὸ σώματον, the earth or the
body. They symbolized the latter by the Virgin.[40] In
this way they added the feminine element to their
physical Trinity, producing thereby the quaternity
or the circulus quadratus, the symbol of which was
the hermaphroditic Rebis, the filius sapientiae. The
medieval philosophers of nature undoubtedly meant
earth and woman by the fourth element. The princi-

ple of evil was not openly mentioned, but it appears
in the poisonous quality of the prima materia and in
other allusions. The quaternity in modern dreams is
a product of the unconscious. As I explained in the
first chapter, the unconscious is often personified by
the anima, a female figure. Apparently the symbol of
the quaternity issues from her. She would be the
matrix of the quaternity, a θεοτόκος or Mater Dei,
just as the earth was understood to be the Mother of
God. But since the woman, as well as evil, is excluded
from the Deity in the dogma of the Trinity, the element of evil would also form a part of the religious
symbol, if the latter should be a quaternity. It needs
no particular effort of imagination to guess the far-
reaching spiritual consequence of such a development

III

THE HISTORY AND PSYCHOLOGY
OF A NATURAL SYMBOL

ALTHOUGH I do not want to discourage philosophical curiosity, I prefer not to lose myself in a discussion of the ethical and intellectual aspects of the problem raised by the quaternity symbol. Its psychological effects are certainly far-reaching and meaningful enough. They play a considerable role in practical treatment. While we are not concerned here with psychotherapy, but with the religious aspect of psychical phenomena, I have been forced through my studies in psychopathology to dig out these historical symbols and figures from the dust of their graves.[1] When I was a young alienist I should never have suspected myself of doing such a thing. I shall not mind, therefore, if this long discussion on the quaternity symbol, the circulus quadratus and the heretical attempts to improve on the dogma of the Trinity seem to be somewhat far fetched and overemphasized. But in point of fact my whole discourse about the quaternity is no more than a regrettably short and inadequate introduction to the final and crowning piece of my paradigmatic case.

Already at the very beginning of our dream series the circle appears. It takes the form, for instance, of a serpent, which describes a circle[2] round the dreamer.

It appears in later dreams as a clock, a circle with a
central point, a round target for shooting practice, a
clock that is a perpetuum mobile, a ball, a globe, a
round table, a basin, and so on. The square appears
also, about the same time, in the form of a town
square or garden with a fountain in the center. Somewhat later the square appears connected with a circular movement:[3] people who walk around in a square,
a magic ceremony (the transformation of animals
into human beings) which takes place in a square
room, in the corners of which are four snakes, and
people are again circulating round the four corners;
the dreamer driving round a square in a taxi; a
square prison cell, an empty square which is itself rotating, and so on. In other dreams the circle is represented by rotation, four children, for instance, carry
a "dark ring" and walk in a circle. The circle appears also combined with the quaternity, as a silver
bowl with four nuts at the four cardinal points; or as
a table with four chairs. The center seems to be particularly emphasized. It is symbolized by an egg in
the middle of a ring; by a star consisting of a body
of soldiers; by a rotating star in a circle, the cardinal
points of which represent the four seasons; by the
pole; or by a precious stone, and so on.

All those dreams lead up to one picture which came
to the patient in the form of a sudden visual impression. He had already had such glimpses or visualiza-
tions on different occasions, but this time it was a
most impressive experience. As he himself says: "It

was an impression of the most sublime harmony." In such a case it does not matter at all what *our* impression is or what *we* think about it. It only matters how the patient feels about it. It is *his* experience, and if it has a deeply transforming influence upon his condition there will be no use arguing against it. The psychologist can only take note of the fact and, if he feels equal to the task, he might also make an attempt to understand why such a vision had such an effect upon such a person. The vision was a turning point in the patient's psychological development. It was what one would call—in the language of religion— a conversion.

This is the literal text of the vision:

"There are a vertical and a horizontal circle with a center common to both. This is the world clock. It is carried by the black bird. [The patient refers here to a preceding vision, where a black eagle had carried away a golden ring.] The vertical circle is a blue disk with a white rim, divided into $4 \times 8 = 32$ partitions. A hand is rotating upon it. The horizontal circle consists of four colors. Four little men are standing upon the circle carrying pendula and the golden ring [of the former vision] is laid around it.

"The world clock has three rhythms or pulses:

"1. The small pulse: the hand of the blue vertical disk moves on one thirty-second (1/32) at a time.

"2. The middle pulse is one complete rotation of the hand. At the same time the horizontal circle moves on by one thirty-second.

"3. The great pulse: thirty-two middle pulses are equal to one complete rotation of the golden ring."

The vision sums up all the allusions in the previous dreams. It seems to be an attempt to make a meaningful whole from the formerly fragmentary symbols, then characterized as circle, globe, square, rotation, clock, star, cross, quaternity, time, and so on.

It is of course difficult to understand why a feeling of "most sublime harmony" should be produced by this abstract structure. But if we think of the two circles in Plato's *Timaeus*, and of the harmonious all-roundness of his anima mundi, we might find an avenue leading to an understanding. Again, the term "world clock" suggests the antique conception of the musical harmony of the spheres. It would be a sort of cosmological system. If it were a vision of the firmament and its silent rotation, or of the steady movement of the solar system, we would readily understand and appreciate the perfect harmony of the picture. We might also assume that the platonic vision of the cosmos was faintly glimmering through the mist of a semiconscious mental condition. But there is something in the vision that does not quite agree with the harmonious perfection of the platonic picture. The two circles are different in nature. Not only is their movement different, but their color, too. The vertical circle is blue and the horizontal one containing four colors is golden. The blue circle might easily symbolize the blue hemisphere of the sky, while the horizontal circle would represent the horizon with the

four cardinal points, personified by the four little
men and characterized by the four colors. (In a
former dream, the four points were represented once
by four children and again by the four seasons.)
This picture reminds one immediately of medieval
representations of the world in the form of a circle or
of the rex gloriae with the four evangelists or of the
melothesiae, where the horizon is formed by the zodiac. The representation of the triumphant Christ
seems to be derived from similar pictures of Horus
and his four sons.[4] There are also Eastern analogies:
the Buddhistic mandalas or circles, usually of Thibetan origin. They consist as a rule of a circular
padma or lotus which contains a square sacred building with four gates, indicating the four cardinal
points and the seasons. The center contains a Buddha
or more often the conjunction of Shiva and his Shakti
or an equivalent dorje (thunderbolt) symbol.[5] They
are yantras or instruments of ritual for the purpose
of contemplation, concentration and the final transformation of the yogin's consciousness into the divine
all-consciousness.[6]

No matter how striking these analogies are, they
are not satisfactory, because they all emphasize the
center to such an extent that they seem to have been
made in order to express the importance of the central figure. In our case, however, the center is empty.
It consists only of a mathematical point. The parallels mentioned depict the world-creating or world-rul-
ing deity, or else man in his dependence upon the ce-

lestial constellations. Our symbol is a clock, symboliz-
ing time. The only analogy to such a symbol that I
can think of is the design of the horoscope. It also has
four cardinal points and an empty center. There is,
moreover, another peculiar coincidence: rotation is
often mentioned in the previous dreams and this is
usually reported as moving to the left. The horoscope
has twelve houses that progress to the left, that is,
anticlockwise.

But the horoscope consists of one circle only and
moreover contains no contrast between two obviously
different systems. Thus the horoscope is also an un-
satisfactory analogy, though it sheds some light upon
the time aspect of our symbol. We should be forced to
give up our endeavor to find psychological parallels
if it were not for the treasure house of medieval symbolism. By good chance I became acquainted with a
little-known medieval author of the early fourteenth
century, Guillaume de Digulleville, the prior of a
monastery at Châlis, a Norman poet, who wrote three
"pélerinages" between 1330 and 1355.[7] They are
called *Le Pélerinage de la Vie Humaine, de l'Âme et
de Jésus Christ.* In the last *Chant du Pélerinage de
l'Âme* we find a vision of paradise.

Paradise consists of forty-nine rotating spheres.
They are called "siècles," centuries, being the proto-
types or archetypes of the earthly centuries. But, as
the angel who serves as a guide to Guillaume explains, the ecclesiastical expression "in saecula saecu-
lorum" means eternity and not ordinary time. A

golden heaven surrounds all the spheres. When Guillaume looked up to the golden heaven he suddenly became aware of a small circle, only three feet wide and of the color of sapphire. He says of this circle: "Il sortait du ciel d'or en un point et y rentrait d'autre part et il en faisait tout le tour." Obviously the blue circle was rolling like a disk upon a great circle which dissected the golden sphere of heaven.

Here then we have two different systems, the one golden, the other blue, and the one cutting through the other. What is the blue circle? The angel again explains to the wondering Guillaume:

> "Ce cercle que tu vois est le calendrier,
> Qui en faisant son tour entier,
> Montre des Saints les journées
> Quand elles doivent être fêtées.
> Chacun en fait le cercle un tour,
> Chacune étoile y est pour jour,
> Chacun soleil pour l'espace
> De jours trente ou zodiaque."

The blue circle is the ecclesiastical calendar. Thus we have here another parallel—the element of time. It will be remembered that time, in our vision, is characterized or measured by three pulses. Guillaume's calendar circle is three feet in diameter. Moreover, while Guillaume is gazing at the blue circle, three spirits clad in purple suddenly appear. The angel explains that this is the moment of the feast of those three saints, and he goes on discoursing about the

whole zodiac. When he comes to the fishes he mentions the feast of the twelve fishermen, which precedes
the Holy Trinity. Here Guillaume breaks in and tells
the angel that he has never quite understood the symbol of the Trinity. He asks him to be good enough to
explain this mystery. Whereupon the angel answers:
"Or, il y a trois couleurs principales: le vert, le rouge
et l'or." One can see them united in the peacock's
tail. And he adds: "Le roi de toute puissance qui met
trois couleurs en unité, ne peut-il faire aussi qu'une
substance soit trois?" The golden color, he says, belongs to the Father, the red to the Son and the green
to the Holy Ghost. Then the angel warns the poet not
to ask any more questions and disappears.

We know, happily enough, from the angel's teaching, that the three has to do with the Trinity. And
thus we know also that our former digression into the
field of mystical speculation about the Trinity has
not been far off the mark. At the same time we meet
the motive of the colors, but unfortunately our patient has four, while Guillaume, or rather the angel,
speaks of three only, gold, red and green. We might
quote the first words of *Timaeus* here: "There are
three, where has the fourth remained?" Or we may
quote the very same words from Goethe's *Faust*, from
the famous scene of the Kabires in Part II, where
they bring up the vision of that mysterious "streng
Gebilde," perhaps to be rendered by "severe image,"
from the sea.

The four little men of our vision are dwarfs or

Kabires. They represent the four cardinal points and the four seasons, as well as the four colors. In *Timaeus* as also in *Faust* and in the *Pélerinage*, the number four is missing. The absent color is obviously blue. It is the one that belongs in the series of yellow, red and green. Why is blue missing? What is wrong with the calendar? or with time? or with the blue color?

Poor old Guillaume has surely stumbled over the same problem: There are three, but where is the fourth? He was indeed eager to hear something about the Trinity which, as he says, he had never quite understood. And it is somewhat suspicious that the angel is in a hurry to get away before Guillaume asks some more awkward questions.

Well, I suppose Guillaume was unconscious when he went to heaven, otherwise he surely would have drawn certain conclusions from what he saw. Now what did he actually see? First he saw the spheres or "siècles" inhabited by those who had attained eternal bliss. Then he beheld the heaven of gold, the "ciel d'or" and there was the King of Heaven, sitting upon a golden throne and, beside him, the Queen of Heaven, sitting upon a round throne of brown crystal. This latter detail refers to the fact that Maria is assumed to have been taken to heaven with her body, as the only mortal being permitted to unite with the body before the resurrection of the dead. In such representations the king is usually the triumphant Christ in conjunction with the church as his bride. But the all-important thing is that the king, being Christ, is at the same time the Trinity, and that the number four is his queen. Blue is the color of Maria's celestial cloak; she is the earth covered by the blue tent of the sky.[8] But why should the Mother of God not be mentioned? According to the dogma she is only beata, and not divine. Moreover, she represents the earth, which is also the body and its darkness. That is the reason why she, the all merciful, is the attorney pleading for all sinners.

From this precious piece of medieval psychology we gain some insight into the merits of our patient's mandala. It unites the four and they function together harmoniously. My patient had been brought up a Catholic and thus, unwittingly, he was confronted with the same problem which caused not a little worry to old Guillaume. It was a great problem indeed to the Middle Ages, that problem of the Trinity and the exclusion, or the very conditioned recognition, of the female element, the earth and the body, which were yet, in the form of Maria's womb, the sacred abode of the Deity and the indispensable link in the chain of the divine work of redemption. My patient's vision is a symbolic answer to the question of the centuries. That is probably the deeper reason why the image of the world clock produced the impression of "most sublime harmony." It was the first intimation of a possible solution of the devastating conflict between matter and spirit, between the desires of the flesh and the love of God. The miserable and ineffectual compromise of the church dream is completely overcome by this mandala vision, in which all contrasts are reconciled. If we are allowed to adduce here the old Pythagorean idea that the soul is a square,[9] the mandala would express the Deity through the threefold rhythm and the soul through the static quaternity, that is, the circle divided into four colors. And thus its innermost meaning would simply be the union of the soul with God.

In as much as the world clock also represents the quadratura circuli and the perpetuum mobile, those two preoccupations of the medieval mind find their adequate expression in our mandala. The golden ring and its contents represent the quaternity in the form of the four Kabires and the four colors, the blue circle the Trinity and the movement of time, according to Guillaume. In our case, the hand of the blue circle has the fastest movement, while the golden circle moves slowly. Whereas the blue circle seems to be somewhat incongruous in Guillaume's golden heaven, the circles in our case are harmoniously combined. The Trinity is now the life, the "pulse" of the whole system, with a threefold rhythm, based, however, on thirty-two, a multiple of four. Thus circle and quaternity on the one side and the threefold rhythm on the other side interpenetrate each other so that the one is also contained in the other. In Guillaume's version, the Trinity is obvious, but the quaternity is concealed in the duality of the King and Queen of Heaven. And moreover the blue color does not adhere to the queen, but to the calendar which represents time, characterized by Trinitarian attributes. This seems to be matter of an interpenetration similar to our case.

Interpenetrations of qualities and contents are typical of symbols. We find this, also, in the Christian Trinity, where the Father is contained in the Son, the Son in the Father and the Holy Ghost contained in Father and Son or penetrating both. The progression from Father to Son represents a time element, while the spatial element would be personified by the Mater Dei. (The mother quality was originally attributed to the Holy Ghost and the latter was then called Sophia-Sapientia by certain early Christians.[10] This female quality could not be completely uprooted, it still adheres, at least, to the symbol of the Holy Ghost, the columba spiritus sancti.) But the quaternity is entirely absent from the dogma, though it appears early in ecclesiastical symbolism. I refer to the cross of equal branches included in the circle, the triumphant Christ with the four evangelists, the Tetramorphus, and so on. In later church symbolism the rosa mystica, the vas devotionis, the fons signatus and the hortus conclusus appear as attributes of the Mater Dei and of the spiritualized earth.[11]

Our mandala is an abstract, almost mathematical representation of some of the main problems abundantly discussed in medieval Christian philosophy. The abstraction goes so far, indeed, that if it had not been for the help of Guillaume's vision we might have overlooked its widespread, historical system of roots. The patient does not possess any real knowledge of such historical materials. He knows only what anybody who received some slight instruction about religion in early childhood would know. He himself saw no connection between his world clock and any religious symbolism. One can readily understand this, since the vision contains nothing that would remind anyone of religion at first sight. Yet the vision itself came shortly after the dream of the "house of self-collection." And that dream again was the answer to the problem of three and four, represented in a still earlier dream. It was a matter there of a rectangular space, on the four sides of which were four goblets filled with colored water. One was yellow, another red, the third green and the fourth was without color. The blue is obviously lacking, yet it had been connected with the three other colors in a previous vision, where a bear appeared in the depth of a cavern. The bear had four eyes emitting red, yellow, green and blue light. Astonishingly enough, in the later dream the blue color had disappeared. At the same time the usual square was transformed into a rectangle, which had never appeared before. The cause of this manifest disturbance was a resistance against the female element represented by the anima. In the dream of the "house of self-collection" the voice confirms this fact. It says: "What thou art doing is dangerous. Religion is not the tax that thou payest in order to get rid of the woman's image, for this image is indispensable." The "woman's image" is exactly what one would call "anima."[12]

It is normal for a man to resist his anima because she represents, as I said before, the unconscious with all those tendencies and contents hitherto excluded from conscious life. They were excluded for a number of real and apparent reasons. Some are suppressed and some are repressed. As a rule those tendencies that represent the amount of antisocial elements in man's psychical structure—what I call the "statistical criminal" in everybody—are suppressed, that is, consciously and deliberately disposed of. But tendencies that are merely repressed are usually only doubtful in character. They are not indubitably antisocial, but are rather unconventional and socially awkward. The reason why one represses them is equally doubtful. Some people repress them from sheer cowardice, others from a merely conventional morality, and others again from the motive of respectability. Repression is a sort of half-conscious and half-hearted letting go of things, a dropping of hot cakes or a reviling of grapes which hang too high, or a looking the other way in order not to become conscious of one's desires. Freud has discovered repression as one of the main mechanisms in the making of a neurosis. Suppression amounts to a conscious moral choice, but repression is a rather immoral "penchant" for getting rid of disagreeable decisions.

Suppression may cause worry, conflict and suffering, but never causes a neurosis of one of the usual patterns. Neurosis is a substitute for legitimate suffering.

If one excludes the "statistical criminal," there remains the vast domain of inferior qualities and of primitive tendencies which belong to the psychical structure of a man who is less ideal and more primitive than we should like to be.[18] We have certain ideas as to how a civilized or educated or moral being should live and we occasionally do our best to fulfil these ambitious expectations. But as nature has not bestowed the same blessings upon each of her children, some are more, and others less, gifted. Thus there are people who can just afford to live properly and respectably, that is, no manifest flaw is discoverable. They either commit minor sins, if they sin at all, or their sins are concealed even to their consciousness. One is rather lenient with sinners unconscious of their sins. Although the law occasionally punishes unconsciousness, the practice of confession in the church is concerned only with deeds which you yourself connect with a feeling of sinfulness. But nature is not at all lenient with unconscious sinners. She punishes them just as severely as if they had committed a conscious offense. Thus we find, as the pious old Drummond once observed, that it is highly moral people, unaware of their other side, who develop peculiar irritability and hellish moods which make them insupportable to their relatives. The fame of saintliness may be far reaching, but to live with a saint might cause an inferiority complex or even a wild outburst of immorality in individuals less morally gifted. Morality seems to be a gift like intelligence. You cannot pump it into a system where it is not indigenous, though you may spoil it.

Unfortunately there is no doubt about the fact that man is, as a whole, less good than he imagines himself or wants to be. Everyone carries a shadow, and the less it is embodied in the individual's conscious life, the blacker and denser it is.[14] If an inferiority is conscious, one always has a chance to correct it. Furthermore, it is constantly in contact with other interests, so that it is steadily subjected to modifications. But if it is repressed and isolated from consciousness, it never gets corrected. It is, moreover, liable to burst forth in a moment of unawareness. At all events, it forms an unconscious snag, blocking the most well meant attempts.

We carry our past with us, to wit, the primitive and inferior man with his desires and emotions, and it is only by a considerable effort that we can detach ourselves from this burden. If it comes to a neurosis, we have invariably to deal with a considerably intensified shadow. And if such a case wants to be cured it is necessary to find a way in which man's conscious personality and his shadow can live together.

This is a very serious problem for all those who are either themselves in such a predicament, or who have to help other people to live. A mere suppression of the shadow is just as little of a remedy as is behead-

ing against headache. To destroy a man's morality
does not help either, because it would kill his better
self, without which even the shadow makes no sense.
The reconciliation of these opposites is a major problem, and even in antiquity it bothered certain minds.
Thus we know of an otherwise legendary personality
of the second century, Karpokrates, a Gnostic,[15] that
he interpreted Matthew 5.25, which reads, "Agree
with thine adversary quickly, whilst thou art in the
way with him," to mean: The adversary is the so-
matic man. As the living body is an indispensable
part of the personality, the text, therefore, should be
read: "Agree with thyself quickly, whilst thou art in
the way with thyself." It is natural that the more
robust mentality of the Fathers could not appreciate
the delicacy and the merit of this subtle and, from a
modern point of view, immensely practical argument.
It was also dangerous, and it is still the most vital
and yet the most ticklish problem of a civilization
that has forgotten why man's life should be sacrificial, that is, offered up to an idea greater than man.
Man can live amazing things if they make sense to
him. But the difficulty is to create that sense. It must
be a conviction naturally; but you find that the most
convincing things man can invent are cheap and
ready made, and never able to convince him against
his personal desires and fears.

If the repressed tendencies, the shadow as I call
them, were decidedly evil, there would be no problem
whatever. But the shadow is merely somewhat infe-

rior, primitive, unadapted, and awkward; not wholly bad. It even contains inferior, childish or primitive qualities which would in a way vitalize and embellish human existence, but "it is not done." The educated public, the flower of our actual civilization, has lifted itself up from its roots and is about to lose its connection with the earth. There is no civilized country nowadays where the lower strata of the population are not in a state of unrest and dissent. In a number of European nations such a condition is overtaking the upper strata, too. This state of affairs is the demonstration of our psychological problem on a gigantic scale. In as much as collectivities are mere accumulations of individuals, their problems are also accumulations of individual problems. One set of people identifies itself with the superior man and cannot descend, and the other set identifies itself with the inferior man and wants to reach the surface.

Such problems are never solved by legislation or tricks. They are only solved by a general change of attitude. And the change does not begin with propaganda and mass meetings, or with violence. It begins with a change in individuals. It will continue as a transformation of their personal likes and dislikes, of their outlook on life and of their values, and only the accumulation of such individual changes will produce a collective solution.

The educated man tries to repress the inferior one in himself, without realizing that by this he forces the latter to become revolutionary. It is characteristic of

my patient that he once dreamt of a military detachment which intended "to strangle the left wing completely." Somebody remarks that the left wing is already weak, but the military detachment answers
that that is the reason why the left wing should be
completely strangled. The dream shows how my patient dealt with his own inferior man. This is clearly
not the right method. The dream of the "house of
self-collection," on the contrary, shows a religious attitude as the correct answer to his question. The mandala seems to be an amplification of this particular
point. Historically, as we have seen, the mandala
served as a symbol in order to clarify the nature of
the deity philosophically, or to demonstrate the same
thing in a visible form for the purpose of adoration,
or, as in the East, as a yantra for yoga practices.
The wholeness of the celestial circle and the squareness of the earth, uniting the four principles or elements or psychical qualities,[16] express completeness
and union. Thus the mandala has the dignity of a
"reconciling symbol."[17] As the reconciliation of God
and man is expressed in the symbol of Christ or of the
cross, we could expect the patient's world clock to
have some similar reconciling significance. Being
prejudiced by historical analogies, we should expect
a deity to occupy the center of the mandala. The center is, however, empty. The seat of the deity is un-
occupied, in spite of the fact that, if we analyze the
mandala according to historical models, we arrive at
the god symbolized by the circle and the goddess

symbolized by the square. Instead of "goddess" we could also say "earth" or "soul." Against the historical prejudice, however, the fact must be insisted upon that (as in the "house of self-collection," where the place of the divine image was occupied by the quaternity) we find no trace of a deity in the mandala. It is, on the contrary, a mechanism. I do not believe that we have any right to disregard such an important fact in favor of a preconceived idea. A dream or a vision is just what it ought to be. It is not a disguise for something else. It is a natural product, which is precisely a thing without ulterior motive. I have seen many hundreds of mandalas, of patients who were quite uninfluenced, and I have found the same fact in an overwhelming majority of cases: there was never a deity occupying the center. The center is emphasized as a rule. But what we find there is a symbol of a very different meaning. It is a star, a sun, a flower, a cross of equal branches, a precious stone, a bowl filled with water or wine, a serpent coiled up, or a human being, but never a god.

When we find a triumphant Christ in the rose window of a medieval church, we assume rightly that this must be a central symbol of the Christian cult. At the same time we also assume that any religion which is rooted in the history of a people is as much an expression of their psychology as the form of political government, for instance, that the people have developed. If we apply the same method to the modern mandalas that people have seen in dreams or visions, or have developed through "active imagination," we reach the conclusion that the mandalas are expressions of a certain attitude which we cannot avoid calling "religious." Religion is a relationship to the highest or strongest value, be it positive or negative. The relationship is voluntary as well as involuntary, that is, you can accept, consciously, the value by which you are possessed unconsciously. That psychological fact which is the greatest power in your system is the god, since it is always the overwhelming psychic factor which is called god. As soon as a god ceases to be an overwhelming factor, he becomes a mere name. His essence is dead and his power is gone. Why have the antique gods lost their prestige and their effect upon human souls? It was because the Olympic gods had served their time and a new mystery began: God became man.

If we allow ourselves to draw conclusions from modern mandalas we should ask people, first, whether they worship stars, suns, flowers or snakes. They will deny it and at the same time they will assert that the globes, stars, crosses and the like are symbols for a center in themselves. And if asked what they mean by that center, they will begin to stammer and to refer to this or that experience which may be something very similar to the confession of my patient who found that the vision of his world clock had left him with a wonderful feeling of perfect harmony. Others will confess that a similar vision came to them in a moment of supreme pain and distress. To others again it is a remembrance of a sublime dream or of a moment when long and fruitless worries came to an end and a reign of peace began. If you sum up what people tell you about their experience, you can formulate it about in this way: They came to themselves, they could accept themselves, they were able to become reconciled to themselves and by this they were also reconciled to adverse circumstances and events. This is much like what was formerly expressed by saying: He has made his peace with God, he has sacrificed his own will, he has submitted himself to the will of God.

A modern mandala is an involuntary confession of a peculiar mental condition. There is no deity in the mandala, and there is also no submission or reconciliation to a deity. The place of the deity seems to be taken by the wholeness of man.[18]

When one speaks of man, everybody means his own ego personality—that is, his personality in as much as he is aware of it—and when one speaks of others one assumes that they have a very similar personality. But since modern research has acquainted us with the fact that an individual consciousness is based upon and surrounded by an indefinitely extended unconscious psyche, we needs must revise our somewhat old-fashioned prejudice that man is his consciousness. This rather naïve assumption must be confronted at once by the critical question: Whose consciousness? Is it his consciousness or the consciousness of other people about him? The fact is that it would be a diffi-

cult task to reconcile the picture I have of myself to
the one which other people make of me. Who is right?
And who is the real individual? When we go further
and take into account the fact that man is also what
neither he himself nor other people know of him—an
unknown something which can yet be proved to exist
—the problem of identity becomes more difficult still.
As a matter of fact it is quite impossible to define the
extension and the ultimate character of psychic existence. When we now speak of man we mean the indefinable whole of him, an ineffable totality, which
can only be formulated symbolically. I have chosen
the term "self" to designate the totality of man, the
sum total of conscious and unconscious existence.[19] I
have chosen this term in accordance with Eastern
philosophy,[20] which for centuries has occupied itself
with those problems that arise when even the gods
cease to become human. The philosophy of the Upan-
ishads corresponds to a psychology that long ago recognized the relativity of the gods.[21] This is not to be
confounded with such a stupid error as atheism. The
world is as it ever has been, but our consciousness undergoes peculiar changes. First, in remote times
(which can, however, still be observed with living
primitives), the main body of psychical life was apparently in human and in nonhuman objects: it was
projected, as we should say now.[22] Consciousness can
hardly exist in a state of complete projection. At
most it would be nothing but a heap of emotions.
Through the withdrawal of projections, conscious

knowledge slowly developed. Science, curiously enough, practically began with the discovery of astronomical laws, which was a first stage in the despiritualization of the world. One step slowly followed another. Already in antiquity they removed the gods from mountains and rivers, from trees and animals. Our science has subtiliated its projections to an almost unrecognizable degree. But our ordinary psychological life is still swarming with projections. You can find them spread out in the newspapers, books, rumors and in ordinary social gossip. All gaps in actual knowledge are still filled with projections. We are still almost certain we know what other people think or what their true character is. We are convinced that certain people have all the bad qualities we do not know in ourselves or that they live all those vices which could, of course, never be our own. We must still be exceedingly careful in order not to project our own shadows too shamelessly; we are still swamped with projected illusions. If you imagine someone who is brave enough to withdraw these projections, all and sundry, then you get an individual conscious of a pretty thick shadow. Such a man has saddled himself with new problems and conflicts. He has become a serious problem to himself, as he is now unable to say that *they* do this or that, *they* are wrong and *they* must be fought against. He lives in the "house of self-collection." Such a man knows that whatever is wrong in the world is in himself, and if he only learns to deal with his own shadow then he has done something real for the world. He has succeeded in removing an infinitesimal part at least of the unsolved gigantic, social problems of our day. These problems are unwieldy and poisoned by mutual projections. How can anyone see straight when he does not even see himself and that darkness which he himself carries unconsciously into all his dealings?

Modern psychological development leads to a much better understanding as to what man really consists of. The gods first lived in superhuman power and beauty on the top of snow-clad mountains or in the darkness of caves, woods and seas. Later on they drew together into one god, and then that god became man. But the gods in our time assemble in the lap of the ordinary individual and are as powerful and as awe-inspiring as ever, in spite of their new disguise— the so-called psychical functions. Man thinks of himself as holding the psyche in the hollow of his hand. He dreams even of making a science of her. But in reality she is the mother and the maker, the psychical subject and even the possibility of consciousness itself. The psyche reaches so far beyond the boundary line of consciousness that the latter could be easily compared to an island in the ocean. While the island is small and narrow, the ocean is immensely wide and deep, so that if it is a question of space, it does not matter whether the gods are inside or outside. But if the historical process of the despiritualization of the world—the withdrawal of projections—is going on as hitherto, then everything of a divine or demonic character must return to the soul, to the inside of the unknown man. At first the materialistic error seems to be inevitable. Since the throne of god could not be discovered among the galactic systems, the inference was that god had never existed. The second inevitable mistake is psychologism: if god is anything, he must be an illusion derived from certain motives, from fear, for instance, from will to power, or from repressed sexuality. These arguments are not new. Similar things have already been said by the Christian missionaries who overthrew the idols of the pagan gods. But whereas the early missionaries were conscious of serving a new God by combatting the old ones, modern iconoclasts are unconscious of the one in whose name they are destroying old values. Nietzsche was quite conscious and quite responsible in breaking the old tablets and yet he felt the peculiar need to back himself up by a revivified Zarathustra as a kind of secondary personality, a sort of alter ego, with whom he often identifies himself in his great tragedy *Thus Spake Zarathustra*. Nietzsche was no atheist, but his God was dead. The result was that Nietzsche himself split and he felt himself forced to call the other self "Zarathustra" or, at other times, "Dionysos." In his fatal illness he signed his letters "Zagreus," the dismembered Dionysos of the Thracians. The tragedy of *Zarathustra* is that, because his God died, Nietzsche himself became a god; and this happened because he was no atheist. He was too positive a nature to content himself with a negative creed. For such a man it seems to be dangerous to make the statement that God is dead. He becomes instantly a victim of "inflation."[23] Since the idea of God represents an important, even overwhelming, psychical intensity, it is, in a way, safer to believe that such an autonomous intensity is a nonego, perhaps an altogether different or superhuman entity, "totaliter-aliter." Confronted with such a belief man must needs feel small, just about his own size. But if he declares the "tremendum" to be dead, then he should find out at once where this considerable energy, which was once invested in an existence as great as God, has disappeared to. It might reappear under another name, it might call itself "Wotan" or "State" or something ending with -ism, even atheism, of which people believe, hope and expect just as much as they formerly did of God. If it does not appear under the disguise of a new name, then it will most certainly return in the mentality of the one from whom the death declaration has issued. Since it is a matter of a tremendous energy, the result will be an equally important psychological disturbance in the form of a dissociation of personality. The disruption can produce a dual or a multiple personality. It is as if one single person could not carry the total amount of energy, so that parts of the personality which were hitherto functional units instantly break asunder and assume the dignity and importance of autonomous personalities.

Happily enough for the rest of mankind, there are not many individuals as sensitive and as religious as

Nietzsche. If dull people lose the idea of God nothing happens—not immediately and personally at least. But socially the masses begin to breed mental epidemics, of which we have now a fair number.

The experience formulated by the mandala is typical of people who cannot project the divine image any longer. They are in actual danger of inflation and dissociation. The round or square inclosures, therefore, have the value of magic means to produce protective walls or a vas hermeticum to prevent an outburst and a disintegration. Thus the mandala denotes and supports an exclusive concentration upon oneself. This state is anything but egocentricity. It is on the contrary a much needed self-control with the purpose of avoiding inflation and dissociation.

The inclosure, as we have seen, has also the meaning of what is called in Greek a τέμενος, the precincts of a temple or any isolated sacred place. The circle, in this case, protects or isolates an inward process that should not become mixed with things outside. Thus the mandala repeats symbolically archaic ways and means which were formerly concrete realities. As I have already mentioned, the inhabitant of the temenos was the god. But the prisoner, or the well-protected dweller in the mandala, does not seem to be a god, in as much as the symbols used, stars, for instance, crosses, globes, and so on do not mean a god, but rather an apparently most important part of the human personality. One might almost say that man himself, or at least his innermost soul, was the prisoner or the protected inhabitant of the mandala. Since modern mandalas have amazingly close parallels in ancient magic circles, in the center of which we usually find the deity, it is evident that in the modern mandala man—the complete man—has replaced the deity.

It is a remarkable fact that this replacement is a natural and spontaneous occurrence and that it is always essentially unconscious. If we want to know what is going to happen in a case where the idea of god is no longer projected as an autonomous entity, this is the answer of man's unconscious mind: The unconscious produces a new idea of man in loco dei, of man deified or divine, imprisoned, concealed, protected, usually dehumanized and expressed by abstract symbolism. The symbols often allude to the medieval conception of the microcosm as well as of the macrocosm, as was the case with my patient's world clock for instance.

It is also a remarkable fact that many of the processes which lead to the mandala, and the latter itself, seem to be direct confirmations of medieval speculations. It looks as if people had read the old tracts about the Philosopher's Stone, the aqua permanens, the divine water, the roundness, the squareness, the four colors and so on. And yet they have never been anywhere near alchemistic philosophy and its abstruse symbolism.

It is difficult to appreciate such facts properly. They could be explained as a regression to archaic

ways of thinking, if one's chief consideration was
their obvious and impressive parallelism with medieval symbolism. But where it is a matter of a regression to an archaic modus, the result is an inferior
adaptation and a corresponding lack of efficiency.
Such a result, however, is by no means typical of
such developments. On the contrary, neurotic and
dissociated conditions improve considerably and the
whole character of people undergoes a change for the
better. Adaptation is rather improved and is not in-
jured in any way. For these reasons, I think, the
process in question should not be explained as a regression. I am rather inclined to understand it as a
true continuation of a psychological process, which
began in the early Middle Ages, and perhaps even
further back, in the times of early Christianity. There
is documentary evidence of essential symbols being
existent in the first century. I speak of the Greek
tract of "Komarios, the archpriest, teaching Kleo-
patra the divine art."[24] The text is indubitably pagan
and of Egyptian origin. There are also the mystical
texts of Zosimos, a Gnostic of the third century.[25]
Here, however, Jewish and Christian influences become noticeable, though the main symbolism is clearly
pagan and is closely connected with the philosophy of
the *Corpus Hermeticum*.[26]

The fact that the symbolism connected with the
mandala traces its near relatives back to pagan
sources casts a peculiar light upon these apparently
modern psychological occurrences. They seem to con-

tinue a Gnostic trend of thought without being supported by direct tradition. If I am right in assuming that every religion is a spontaneous expression of a certain predominant psychological condition, then Christianity was the formulation of a condition that predominated in the beginning of our era and that was valid for many subsequent centuries. But it expressed one condition predominant just then, which does not exclude the existence of other conditions that are equally capable of religious expression. Christianity had to fight for its life for awhile against Gnosticism which, for all we know, was another condition almost tantamount to the "Christian" precondition. Gnosticism was stamped out completely and its remnants are so badly mangled that special study is needed to get any insight at all into its inner meaning. But if the historical roots of our symbols extend beyond the Middle Ages they are certainly to be found in Gnosticism.

It would not be altogether illogical, I must admit, if a psychological condition, previously suppressed, should reassert itself when the main ideas of the suppressing condition begin to subside. In spite of the suppression of the Gnostic heresy it continued throughout the Middle Ages under the disguise of alchemy. It is a well-known fact that the latter consisted of two parts indispensable to each other—on the one side the chemical research proper and on the other the "theoria" or "philosophia." As the title of the writings of Pseudo-Demokritos belonging to the

first century τὰ φυσικὰ καὶ τὰ μυστικά denotes,[27] the two
aspects already went together in the beginning of our
era. The same holds true of the Leyden papyri and
the writings of Zosimos of the third century. The religious or philosophical views of antique alchemy were
clearly Gnostic. The later views seem to cluster round
a peculiar, unclear idea. It could perhaps be formulated in the following way: The anima mundi, the
demiurge or the divine spirit that incubated the chaotic waters of the beginning, remained in matter in a
potential state, and the primary chaotic condition
persisted with it.[28] Thus the philosophers, or the "sons
of wisdom" as they called themselves, took their famous prima materia to be a part of the original chaos
pregnant with the spirit. By "spirit" they understood a semimaterial pneuma, a sort of "subtle body,"
which they also called "volatile" and identified chemically with oxides and other dissoluble compounds.
They called the spirit Mercury, which was chemically
quicksilver and philosophically Hermes, the god of
revelation, who, as Hermes Trismegistos, was the
arch-authority of alchemy.[29] Their intention was to
extract the original divine spirit out of the chaos,
which extract was called quinta essentia, aqua permanens, ὕθωρ θεῖον, βαφή or tinctura. A famous al-
chemist, Johannes de Rupescissa (1378)[30] calls the
quintessence "le ciel humain," the human sky or
heaven. To him it was a blue liquid and incorruptible
like the sky. He says that the quintessence is of the
color of the sky "et notre soleil l'a orné, tout ainsi

que le soleil orne le ciel." The sun is an allegory of
gold. He says: "Iceluy Soleil est vray or." He continues: "Ces deux choses conjointes ensemble, influ-
ent en nous . . . les conditions du Ciel des cieux, et
du Soleil céleste." His idea is, obviously, that the
quintessence, the blue sky and the golden sun therein,
produce the images of the heaven and of the heavenly
sun in ourselves. It is a picture of a blue and golden
microcosm,[31] which I understand as a direct parallel
to Guillaume's celestial vision. The colors are, however, reversed; with Rupescissa the disk is golden and
the heaven blue. My patient therefore, having a similar arrangement, seems to be more on the alchemistic
side.

The miraculous liquid, the divine water, called sky
or heaven, probably refers to the "supra-celestial
waters" of Genesis 1.6. In its functional aspect it was
thought to be a sort of baptismal water, like the holy
water of the church containing the creative and transforming quality.[32] The Catholic church still performs
the rite of the benedictio fontis on the sabbathum
sanctum before Easter.[33] The rite consists of a repetition of the descensus spiritus sancti in aquam. The
ordinary water acquires thereby the divine quality of
transforming and of giving spiritual rebirth to man.
This is exactly the alchemistic idea of the divine water
and there would be no difficulty whatever in deriving
the aqua permanens of alchemy from the rite of the
benedictio fontis, if the former were not of pagan origin and certainly the older of the two. We find the

miraculous water in the first tracts of Greek alchemy which belong to the first century.[34] Moreover the descensus spiritus into the physis is a Gnostic legend, which had the greatest influence on Mani. And it was possibly through Manichean influences that it became one of the main ideas of Latin alchemy. The intention of the philosophers was to transform imperfect matter chemically into gold, the panacea, or the elixir vitae, but philosophically or mystically into the divine hermaphroditus, the second Adam,[35] the glorified, incorruptible body of resurrection,[36] or the lumen luminum,[37] the illumination of the human mind or the sapientia. As I have shown, together with Richard Wilhelm, Chinese alchemy produced the same idea, that the goal of the opus magnum is the creation of the "diamond body."[38]

All this detail is an attempt to put my psychological observations into their historical setting. Without the historical connection, they would remain suspended in mid-air, a mere curiosity. As I have already pointed out, the connection of modern symbolism with ancient theories and beliefs is not established by the usual direct or indirect tradition, and not even by a secret tradition as has often been surmised.[39] The most careful inquiry has never revealed any possibility of my patients' being acquainted with books or having any other information about such ideas. It seems that their unconscious mind has worked along the same line of thought which has manifested itself, time and again, within the last two thousand years.

Such a continuity can only exist if we assume a certain unconscious condition carried on by biological inheritance. By this assumption I naturally do not mean an inheritance of representations, which would be difficult if not impossible to prove. The inherited quality, I fancy, must rather be something like a possibility of regenerating the same or at least similar ideas. I have called the possibility "archetype," which means a mental precondition and a characteristic of the cerebral function.[40]

In the light of such historical parallels the mandala either symbolizes the divine being, hitherto hidden and dormant in the body and now extracted and revivified, or it symbolizes the vessel or the room in which the transformation of man into a divine being takes place.

I know such formulations remind one fatally of wild metaphysical speculations. I am sorry, but it is exactly what the human mind produces and has always produced. A psychology which assumes that it could do without such facts must artificially exclude them. I should call this a philosophic prejudice, inadmissible from the empirical standpoint. I should emphasize, perhaps, that we do not establish a metaphysical truth through such formulations. It is merely a statement that the mind functions in such a way. And it is a fact that my patient felt a great deal better after the vision of the mandala. If you understand the problem which it has settled for him, you can also understand why he had such a feeling of "sublime harmony."

I should not hesitate for a moment to suppress all speculations about the possible consequences of an experience as abstruse and as remote as the mandala, were this feasible. But to me, unfortunately, this type of experience is neither abstruse nor remote. On the contrary, it is an almost daily concern in my profession. I know a fair number of people who have to take their experience seriously if they want to live at all. They can only choose between the devil and the deep sea. The devil is the mandala or something equivalent to it and the deep sea their neurosis. The devil is at least somewhat heroic, but the sea is spiritual death. The well-meaning rationalist will point out that I am driving out the devil by Baalzebub and that I replace an honest neurosis by the cheat of a religious belief. Concerning the former I have nothing to reply, being no metaphysical expert, but concerning the latter, I must point out that there is no question of belief, but of experience. Religious experience is absolute. It is indisputable. You can only say that you have never had such an experience, and your opponent will say: "Sorry, I have." And there your discussion will come to an end. No matter what the world thinks about religious experience, the one who has it possesses the great treasure of a thing that has provided him with a source of life, meaning and beauty and that has given a new splendor to the world and to mankind. He has pistis and peace. Where is the criterium by which you could say that such a life is not legitimate, that such experience is not valid and that such pistis is mere illusion? Is there, as a matter of fact, any better truth about ultimate things than the one that helps you to live? This is the reason why I take carefully into account the symbols produced by the unconscious mind. They are the only things able to convince the critical mind of modern people. They are convincing for very old-fashioned reasons. They are simply overwhelming, which is an English rendering of the Latin word "convincere." The thing that cures a neurosis must be as convincing as the neurosis; and since the latter is only too real, the helpful experience must be of equal reality. It must be a very real illusion, if you want to put it pessimistically. But what is the difference between a real illusion and a healing religious experience? It is merely a difference in words. You can say, for instance, that life is a disease with a very bad prognosis, it lingers on for years to end with death; or that normality is a generally prevailing constitutional defect; or that man is an animal with a fatally overgrown brain. This kind of thinking is the prerogative of habitual grumblers with bad digestions. Nobody can know what the ultimate things are. We must, therefore, take them as we experience them. And if such experience helps to make your life healthier, more beautiful, more complete and more satisfactory to yourself and to those you love, you may safely say: "This was the grace of God."

NOTES

I

1. Rudolf Otto, *Das Heilige* (1917).

2. The gratia adiuvans and the gratia sanctificans are the effects of the sacramentum ex opere operato. The sacrament owes its efficiency to the fact that it is immediately instituted by Christ himself. The church is unable to connect the rite with grace, so that the actus sacramentalis would produce the presence and the effect of grace, i.e., res et sacramentum. Thus the ritual carried out by the priest is not causa instrumentalis, but merely causa ministerialis.

3. "But our esteem for facts has not neutralized in us all religiousness. It is itself almost religious. Our scientific temper is devout" (William James, *Pragmatism* [1911], p. 14 *et seq.*).

4. "Religio est, quae superioris cujusdam naturae (quam divinam vocant) curam caerimoniamque affert" (Cicero, *De invent. Rhetor.*, Lib. II); "Religiose testimonium dicere ex jurisjurandi fide" (Cicero, *Pro Coel.*, 55).

5. Heinrich Scholz (*Religionsphilosophie*, 1921) insists upon a similar point of view; see also H. R. Pearcy, *A Vindication of Paul* (1936).

6. Jung, *Studies in Word-Association* (London, 1918).

7. J. G. Frazer, *Taboo and the Perils of the Soul* (1911), p. 80 *et seq.*; A. E. Crawley, *The Idea of the Soul* (London, 1909), p. 82 *et seq.*; L. Lévy-Bruhl, *La Mentalité Primitive* (Paris, 1922), *passim*.

8. Feun, *Running Amok* (1901).

9. M. Ninck, *Wodan und germanischer Schicksalsglaube* (Jena, 1935).

10. L. Lévy-Bruhl, *Les Fonctions Mentales dans les Sociétés Inférieures. Idem, Mental. Prim.*, chap. III, "Les Rêves."

11. Fr. Haeussermann, *Wortempfang und Symbol in der alttestamentlichen Prophetie* (Giessen, 1932).

12. In an excellent tract about dreams and their functions Benedictus Pererius, S. J. (*De Magia. De Observatione Somniorum et de Divinatione Astrologica libri tres* [Coloniae Agripp., 1598], p. 114 *et seq.*), says: "Deus nempe, istius modi temporum legibus non est alligatus nec opportunitate temporum eget ad operandum, ubicunque enim vult, quandocumque, et quibuscumque vult, sua

inspirat somnia . . ." (p. 147). The following passage casts an
interesting light on the relation between the church and the problem of dreams: "Legimus enim apud Cassianum in collatione 22.
veteres illos monachorum magistros et rectores, in perquirendis, et
excutiendis quorundam somniorum causis, diligenter esse versatos"
(p. 142). Pererius classifies dreams in the following manner:
"Multa sunt naturalia, quaedam humana, nonnulla etiam divina"
(p. 145). There are four causes of dreams: I. An affection of the
body. II. An affect or vehement commotion of the mind through
love, hope, fear or hatred (p. 126 *et seq.*). III. The power and
cunning of the demon, meaning a pagan god or the Christian
devil. (Potest enim daemon naturales effectus ex certis causis ali-
quando necessario proventuros, potest quaecunque ipsemet postea
facturus est, potest tam prasentia quam praeterita, quae hominibus occulta sunt, cognoscere, et hominibus per somnium indicare
[p. 129].) Concerning the interesting diagnosis of demonic dreams,
the author says: ". . . conjectari potest, quae somnia missa sint
a daemone: primo quidem, si frequenter accidant somnia signifi-
cantia res futuras, aut occultas, quarum cognitio non ad utilitatem
vel ipsius, vel aliorum, sed ad inanem curiosae scientiae ostenta-
tionem, vel etiam ad aliquid mali faciendum conferat . . ." (p.
130). IV. Dreams sent by God. Concerning the signs indicating the
divine nature of a dream the author says: ". . . ex praestantia
rerum, quae per somnium significantur: nimirum, si ea per somnium innotescant homini, quorum certa cognitio, solius Dei con-
cessu ac munere potest homini contingere, hujus modi sunt, quae
vocantur in scolis Theologorum, futura contingentia, arcana item
cordium, quaeque intimis animorum recessibus, ab omni penitus
mortalium intelligentia oblitescunt, denique praecipua fidei nostrae
mysteria, nulli, nisi Deo docente manifesta(!!)" ". . . deinde, hoc
ipsum (divinum esse) maxime declaratur interiori quadam animorum illuminatione atque commotione, qua Deus sic mentem il-
lustrat, sic voluntatem afficit, sic hominem de fide et auctoritate
eius somnii certiorem facit, ut Deum esse ipsius auctorem, ita
perspicue agnoscat et liquido iudicet, ut id sine dubitatione ulla
credere et velit et debeat" (p. 131 *et seq.*). Since the demon, as
mentioned above, is also liable to produce dreams accurately predicting future events, the author adds a quotation from Gregory
(*Dialog.*, Lib. IV, cap. 48): "Sancti viri illusiones atque revela-
tiones, ipsas visionum voces et imagines, quondam intimo sapore
discernunt, ut sciant quid a bono spiritu percipiant et quid ab
illusore patiantur. Nam si erga haec mens hominis cauta non esset,

per deceptorem spiritum, multis se vanitatibus immergeret, qui nonnumquam solet multa vera praedicere, ut ad extremum valeat animam ex una aliqua falsitate laqueare" (p. 132). It seemed to be a welcome safeguard against this uncertainty if dreams occupied themselves with the "main mysteries of our faith." Athanasius, in his biography of St. Anthony, gives us some idea of how clever the devils are in predicting future events (cf. E. A. Wallis Budge, *The Book of Paradise* [London, 1904], I, p. 37 *et seq.*). According to the same author they appear sometimes even in the shape of monks, singing psalms, reading the Bible aloud and making confusing comments about the moral conduct of the brethren (pp. 33 *et seq.*, 47). Pererius, however, seems to trust his criterium and he continues: "Quemadmodum igitur naturale mentis nostrae lumen facit nos evidenter cernere veritatem primorum principiorum, namque statim citra ullam argumentationem, assensu nostro complecti: sic enim somniis a Deo datis, lumen divinum animis nostris affulgens, perficit, ut ea somnia et vera et divina esse intelligamus certoque credamus." Pererius does not touch the dangerous question of whether any unshakable conviction, derived from a dream, necessarily proves the divine origin of the dream. He merely takes it for granted that a dream of this sort would naturally exhibit a character conforming to the "main mysteries of our faith," and not by any chance with those of another one. The humanist Caspar Peucer (in his *Commentarius de Praecipuis Generibus Divinationum,* etc. Witebergae 1560 de divinat. ex somn., p. 270) is far more definite and restrictive in that respect. He says: "Divina somnia sunt, quae divinitus immissa sacrae literae affirmant, non quibusvis promiscue, nec captantibus aut expectantibus peculiares ἀποκαλύψεις sua opinione, sed sanctis Patribus et Prophetis Dei arbitrio et voluntate, nec de levibus negociis, aut rebus nugacibus et momentaneis, sed de Christo, de gubernatione Ecclesiae, de imperiis et eorundem ordine, de aliis mirandis eventibus: et certa his semper addidit Deus testimonia, ut donum interpretationis et alia, quo constaret non temere ea objici ex natura nasci, sed inseri divinitus." His crypto-Calvinism tangibly manifests itself in his words, particularly if they are compared with the theologia naturalis of his Catholic contemporary. It is probable that Peucer's hint at "revelations" alludes to heretical innovations. In the next paragraph at least, where he deals with somnia diabolici generis, he says: "Quaeque nunc Anabaptistis et omni tempore Enthusiastis et similibus fanaticis . . . diabolus exhibet." Pererius with more perspicacity and human understanding devotes a chapter to the question: "An licitum sit christiano homini, observare somnia?" and another one to the question: "Cuius hominis sit rite interpretari somnia?" In the first one he reaches the conclusion that important dreams should be considered. I quote his words: "Denique somnia, quae nos saepe commovent, et incitant ad flagitia, considerare num a daemone nobis subjiciantur, sicut contra, quibus ad bona provocamur et instigamur, veluti ad caelibatum, largitionem eleemosynarum et ingressum in religionem, ea ponderari num a Deo nobis missa sint, non est superstiosi animi, sed religiosi, prudentis ac salutis suae satagentis atque solliciti." But only stupid people would observe all the other futile dreams. In the second chapter he answers that nobody should or could interpret dreams "nisi divinitus afflatus et eruditus." "Nemo enim," he adds, "novit quae Dei sunt, nisi spiritus Dei" (*R. Cor.*, I, 2.11). This statement, eminently true in itself, reserves the art of interpretation to such persons as are ex officio endowed with the donum spiritus sancti. It is obvious, however, that a Jesuit author could not envisage a descensus spiritus sancti extra ecclesiam.

13. Jung, "Traumsymbole des Individuationsprozesses," *Eranos-Jahrbuch 1935* (Zürich, 1936). Although the dreams I quote are mentioned in this publication, they have been examined there from another angle. As dreams have many aspects, they can be studied from different sides.

14. Freud, *Traumdeutung* (Vienna, 1900). Eng. trans., *Interpretation of Dreams*. Herbert Silberer, *Der Traum* (1919), represents a more cautious and a more balanced point of view. Concerning the difference between Freud's and my own views, I refer the reader to my little essay on this subject in *Modern Man in Search of a Soul* (London, 1933), p. 132. Further material in *Two Essays on Analytical Psychology* (1928), p. 83 *et seq.;* W. M. Kranefeldt, *Secret Ways of the Mind* (New York, 1932); Gerhard Adler, *Entdeckung der Seele* (Zürich, 1934); T. Wolff, "Einführung in die Grundlagen der Komplexen Psychologie," *Die Kulturelle Bedeutung der Komplexen Psychologie* (Berlin, 1935), pp. 1–168.

15. Cf. the relation of Odin as a god of poets, seers and raving enthusiasts, and Mimir, the wise one, to Dionysos and Silenos. The word Odin has a root connection with Gall. οὐατεις, Jr. fáith, Lat. Vates, similar to μάντις and μαίνομαι. Martin Ninck, *Wodan und germanischer Schicksalsglaube* (1935), p. 30 *et sqq.*

16. In *Ueber das Unbewusste* (Schweizerland, 1918).

17. In "Wotan," *Neue Schweizer Rundschau*, Heft 11 (1936).

An abbreviated edition in *Saturday Review of Literature* (Oct. 16, 1937). The Wotan parallels in Nietzsche's work are to be found (1) in the poem of 1863-64 "To the Unknown God"; (2) in "Klage der Ariadne," *Also sprach Zarathustra*, p. 366; (3) *Also sprach Zarathustra*, p. 143 and p. 200; (4) The Wotan dream of 1859 in E. Foerster-Nietzsche, *Der werdende Nietzsche* (1924), p. 84 *et sqq*.

18. *Two Essays*, p. 202 *et sqq.; Psychological Types* (1923), pp. 588, 593 *et sqq.;* "Ueber die Archetypen des collectiven Unbewussten," *Eranos-Jahrbuch 1934*, p. 204 *et sqq.;* "Ueber den Archetypus mit besonderer Berücksichtigung des Animabegriffes," *Zentralblatt für Psychotherapie*, IX (1936), 259 *et sqq*.

19. *Zentralbl. f. Psychotherapie*, IX, 259 *et sqq*.

20. Edward Maitland, *Anna Kingsford, Her Life, Letters, Diary and Work* (London, 1896), p. 129 *et seq*.

21. The statement, concerning the hermaphroditic nature of the Deity in *Corpus Hermeticum*, Lib. I (ed. W. Scott, *Hermetica*, I, p. 118: ὁ δὲ νοῦς ὁ πρῶτος ἀρρενόθηλυς ὤν), is probably derived from Plato, *Symposium XIV*. It is questionable whether the later medieval representatives of the hermaphrodite are derived from the "Poimandres" (*Corp. Herm.*, Lib. I) since it was practically unknown in the West before it was printed by Marsilius Ficinus in 1471. There is a possibility, however, that a Greek scholar, though rare in those days, has gleaned the idea from one of the then existing codices graeci, as, for instance, the *Cod. Laurentianus* 71, 33 of the fourteenth century, the *Parisinus Graec.* 1220, fourteenth century, the *Vaticanus Graec.* 237 and 951, fourteenth century. There are no older codices. The first Latin translation by Marsilius Ficinus had a sensational effect. But before that date we have the hermaphroditic symbols of the *Cod. Germ. Monac.*, 598 of 1417. It seems more probable to me that the hermaphroditic symbol is derived from Arabic or Syriac Mss. translated in the eleventh or twelfth century. In the old Latin *Tractatulus Avicennae,* strongly influenced by Arabic tradition, we find: "(Elixir) Ipsum est serpens luxurians, seipsum impraegnans (*Artis Auriferae,* etc. [1593], T. I., p. 406). Although it is matter of a Pseudo-Avicenna and not of the authentic Ibn Sina (970–1037), he belongs to the Arabo-Latin sources of the medieval Hermetic philosophy. We find the same passage in the tractatus "Rosinus ad Sarratantam" (*Art. Aurif.* [1593], I, 309): "Et ipsum est serpens seipsum luxurians, seipsum impraegnans, etc." "Rosinus" is an Arabo-Latin corruption of "Zosimos," the Greek neo-Platonic

philosopher of the third century. His tract *Ad Sarratantam* belongs to the same class of literature and since the history of these texts is still completely in the dark, nobody can say who copied from whom. The *Turba Philosophorum*, Sermo LXV, a Latin text of Arabic origin, also makes the allusion: "compositum germinat se ipsum" (J. Ruska, *Turba Philosophorum. Quellen und Studien zur Geschichte der Naturwissenschaften und der Medizin* [1931], p. 165). As far as I can make out, the first text definitely mentioning the hermaphrodite is the "Liber de Arte Chimica incerti autoris," sixteenth century (in *Art. Aurif.* [1593], I, 575 *et sqq.*), p. 610: "Is vero mercurius est omnia metalla, masculus et foemina, et monstrum Hermaphroditum in ipso animae et corporis matrimonio." Of later literature I mention only: *Pandora* (a German text, 1588); "Splendor Solis" in *Aureum Vellus,* etc. (1598); Michael Majer, *Symbola aureae mensae duodecim nationum* (1617); *idem, Atalanta Fugiens* (1618). J. D. Mylius, *Philosophia Reformata* (1622).

22. The *Tractatus Aureus Hermetis* is of Arabic origin and does not belong to the *Corpus Hermeticum.* Its history is unknown (first printed in the *Ars Chemica,* 1566). Dominicus Gnosius has written a commentary to the text in *Hermetis Trismegisti Tractatus vere Aureus de Lapidis Philosophici Secreto cum Scholiis Dominici Gnosii,* 1610. He says (p. 101): "Quem ad modum in sole ambulantis corpus continuo sequitur umbra . . . sic hermaphroditus noster Adamicus, quamvis in forma masculi appareat semper tamen in corpore occultatam Evam sive foeminam suam secum circumfert." This commentary, together with the text, is reproduced in J. J. Mangeti, *Bibl. Chem.* (1702), I, 401 *et sqq.*

23. A description of both types in *Two Essays,* II, 202 *et sqq.* See also *Psychological Types,* Definition No. 48, p. 588 *et sqq.;* also Emma Jung, "Ein Beitrag zum Problem des Animus," in *Wirklichkeit der Seele* (1934), p. 296 *et sqq.*

II

1. A bishop is allowed to have four candles for a private mass. Certain forms of more solemn masses as, for instance, the missa cantata also have four. Still higher forms have six and seven candles.

2. Origenes, in *Jerem. hom.,* XX, 3.

3. From the Pythagorean oath: Οὐ μὰ τὸν ἀμετέρα γενεᾷ παραδόντα τετρακτὺν, παγὰν ἀενάου φύσιος ῥιζώματ' ἔχουσαν· See E.

Zeller, *Die Philosophie der Griechen* (2d ed., 1856), I, 291, where
all sources are collected. The "four is the origin and root of eternal
nature." Plato derives the body from the "four." According to the
neo-Pythagoreans Pythagoras himself designated the soul as a
square (Zeller, III Th., II Abt., p. 120).

4. The "four" in Christian iconology appears chiefly in the form
of the four evangelists and their symbols, arranged in a "rose,"
circle or melothesia, or as tetramorphus, for instance, in the "hortus
deliciarum" of Herrad von Landsperg, and in works of mystical
speculation: I mention only (1) Jakob Boehme, *XL Questions concerning the Soule propounded by Dr. Balthasar Walter and answered by Jacob Behmen*, etc. (London, 1647) ; (2) Hildegard von
Bingen, *Cod. Lucc.*, fol. 372, *Cod. Heidelb. Scivias*, representation
of the mystical universe; S. Ch. Singer, *Studies in the History and
Method of Science* (1917); (3) the remarkable drawings of Opici-
nus de Canistris, *Cod. Pal. Lat.* 1993, Vatican Libr.; S. R. Salo-
mon, *O.d.C. Weltbild und Bekenntnisse eines avignonensischen
Clerikers des 14 Jahrhunderts*, 1936; (4) Heinrich Khunrath, the
"monas catholica" originates from the rotation of the "quaternarium." The monas is interpreted as an imago and allegoria
Christi (*Vom hylealischen, das ist, primaterialischen Chaos*, 1597,
p. 204 and p. 281. Further material in *Amphiteatrum Sapientiae
Aeternae*, 1608); (5) The speculations about the cross ("de quatuor generibus arborum facta fuisse refertur crux"—Bernardus in
Vitis Mystica, cap. XLVI; S. W. Meyer, *Die Geschichte des Kreuz-
holzes vor Christus*, Abhandl. d. k. bayerisch. Akad. d. Wissen-
schaften [1881], I, Cl. XVI, Bd. II, Abh., p. 7). Concerning quaternity, see also Dunbar, *Symbolism in Medieval Thought and Its
Consummation in the Divine Comedy* (1929), *passim*.

5. I refer to the systems of Isidoros, Valentinos, Markos and
Sekundos. A most instructive example is the symbolism of the
Monogenes in *Cod. Brucianus* (Bruce Ms. 96, Bodleian Libr., Ox-
ford, C. A. Baynes, *A Coptic Gnostic Treatise*, etc. [1933], p. 59
et seq. and p. 70 *et seq.*).

6. I refer to the mystical speculation about the four radices
(Empedocles' ῥιζώματα) = the four elements and the four qualities (humid, dry, warm, cold) peculiar to Hermetic or alchemistic
philosophy. Representations in Janus Lacinius, *Pretiosa Margarita
Novella*, etc. (1546), "Artis metallicae schema," based upon a quaternatio in Joannes Aug. Pantheus, *Ars Transmutationis*, etc.
(1519), p. 5; a quaternatio elementoram and of chemical processes
in Raymundi Lulli, "Practica" (*Theatr. Chem.*, Vol. IV [1613],

p. 174); symbols of the four elements in M. Majer, *Scrutinium Chymicum* (1687). The same author has written an interesting tract, *De Circulo Physico Quadrato* (1616). Similar symbolism in Mylius, *Philosophia Reformata* (1622). Representation of the Hermetic salvation (from *Pandora* [1588] and from *Cod. Germ. Monac.*, No. 598) in form of a tetras with the evangelist symbols in Jung, "Die Erlösungsvorstellungen in der Alchemie," *Eranos-Jahrbuch 1936*, pp. 94, 96. About the symbolism of the "four," *idem*, "Traumsymbole des Individuationsprozesses," *Eranos-Jahrbuch 1935*, p. 54 *et sqq*. Further material in H. Kuekelhaus, *Urzahl und Gebärde* (1934). Eastern parallels in H. Zimmer, *Kunstform und Yoga im Indischen Kultbild* (1926); Wilhelm and Jung, *The Secret of the Golden Flower* (1931). The literature about the cross symbolism also belongs here (Zoeckler, *Das Kreuz Christi* [1875]).

7. Concerning the definition of the unconscious, see *Psychological Types* (1923), p. 613.

8. *Two Essays* (1928), p. 252 *et sqq*.

9. I refer the reader to Claudius Popelin, *Le Songe de Poliphile ou Hypnérotomachie de Frère Francesco Colonna* (Paris, 1883), Vol. II. This book is written by a monk of the fifteenth century. It is an excellent example of an "anima mystery."

10. The vestments not only ornament the celebrating priest, they also protect him.

11. See *Psychological Types*, p. 554 *et sqq*., *s.v.* "Imago."

12. The term "archetypus" is used by Cicero, Pliny and others. It appears in the nature of a clearly philosophical concept in *Corp. Herm.*, Lib. I (W. Scott, *Hermetica*, I, 116: εἶδες ἐν τῷ νῷ τὸ ἀρχέτυπον εἶδος, τὸ προάρχον τῆς ἀρχῆς, τὸ ἀπέραντον . . .).

13. Adolf Bastian, *Das Beständige in den Menschenrassen* (1868), p. 75. *Idem*, "Die Vorstellungen von der Seele" (in Virchow u. Holtzendorff, *Wissenschaftl. Vorträge* [1874], p. 306). *Idem, Der Völkergedanke im Aufbau einer Wissenschaft vom Menschen* (1881). *Idem, Ethnische Elementargedanken in der Lehre vom Menschen* (1895).

14. Nietzsche, *Human, All Too Human*, II, 27: "In our sleep and in our dreams we pass through the whole thought of earlier humanity. I mean, in the same way that man reasons in his dreams, he reasoned when in the waking state many thousands of years. The first *causa* which occurred to his mind in reference to anything that needed explanation, satisfied him and passed for truth. In the dream this atavistic relic of humanity manifests its existence

within us, for it is the foundation upon which the higher rational faculty developed, and which is still developing in every individual. The dream carries us back into earlier states of human culture, and affords us a means of understanding it better."

15. Hubert et Mauss, *Mélanges d'Histoire des Religions* (Paris, 1909), Préface, p. XXIX: "Constamment présentes dans le langage, sans qu'elles y soient de toute nécessité explicites,—les catégories—existent d'ordinaire plutôt sous la forme d'habitudes directrices de la conscience, elles-mêmes inconscientes. La notion de *mana* est un de ces principes: elle est donnée dans le langage; elle est impliquée dans toute une série de jugements et de raisonnements, portant sur des attributs qui sont ceux de mana, nous avons dit que le mana est une catégorie. Mais le mana n'est pas seulement une catégorie spéciale à la pensée primitive, et aujourd'hui, en voie de réduction c'est encore la forme première qu'ont revêtue d'autres catégories qui fonctionnent toujours dans nos esprits: celle de substance et de cause," etc.

16. L. Lévy-Bruhl, *Les Fonctions Mentales dans les Sociétés Inférieures* (M. E. Durkheim, *Travaux de l'Année Sociologique*).

17. *Psychology of the Unconscious* (1927); Wilhelm and Jung, *The Secret of the Golden Flower* (1931); "Traumsymbole des Ind. Proz.," *Eranos-Jahrbuch 1935.*

18. Concerning the psychology of the tetraktys, see *Secret of the Golden Flower*, p. 96 *et sqq.;* "Traumsymbole des Ind. Proz.," *passim* and "The Relation between the Ego and the Unconscious," p. 252 *et sqq.* (*Two Essays* [1928]); Hauer, "Symbole und Erfahrung des Selbstes in der Indo-Arischen Mystik," *Eranos-Jahrbuch 1934*, p. 1 *et sqq.*

19. An excellent presentation of the problem in Michael Majer, *De Circulo Physico Quadrato*, etc. (1616).

20. Plato, *Timaeus*, 7. J. Ch. Steebus, *Coelum Sephiroticum* (1679), p. 15.

21. Steebus, *Coelum Sephiroticum*, p. 19. M. Majer (*De Circulo*, p. 27) says: "circulus aeternitatis symbolum sive punctum indivisibile." Concerning the "round element" cf. *Turba Philosophorum* (ed. Ruska, Sermo XLI, p. 148) where the "rotundum quod aes in quatuor vertit" is mentioned. Ruska says that the Greek sources do not yield a similar symbolism. This is not quite correct, since we find a στοιχεῖον στρογγύλον in Zosimos' περὶ ὀργάνων (Berthelot, *Coll. d. Anciens Alchémistes Grecs.*, III, XLIX, 1). The same symbolism occurs probably also in Zosimos' ποίημα (Berthelot, III, V *bis*) in the form of the περιηκονισμένον which Berthelot trans-

lates "objet circulaire." Berthelot's text has περιηκοννυσμένον, which is impossible. Dr. Guenther Goldschmidt calls my attention to the fact that probably an iota subscriptum has been omitted, which Berthelot has obviously thought too. The same idea of the creative point in matter is mentioned in *Musaeum Hermeticum*, 1678, *Novum Lumen*, p. 559. (Est enim in quolibet corpore centrum et locus, vel seminis seu spermatis punctum.) This point is also designated as scintilla, the soul spark (*loc. cit.*, p. 559). The point is punctum divinitus ortum (*Musaeum*, p. 59). It is matter of the doctrine of "panspermia," about which Athanasius Kircher, S.J. (in *Mundus Subterraneus* [Amsterdam, 1678], p. 347), says: "Ex sacris itaque Mosaicis oraculis . . . constat, conditorem omnium Deum in principio rerum Materiam quandam, quam nos non incongrue Chaoticam appellamus, ex nihilo creasse . . . intra quem quicquid . . . veluti sub πανσπερμία quadam confusum latebat . . . veluti ex subjacente materia et Spiritus divini incubitu jam foecundata postea omnia . . . eduxerit. . . . Materiam vero Chaoticam non statim abolevit, sed usque ad Mundi consummationem durare voluit, uti in primordiis rerum, ita in hunc usque diem, panspermia omnium rerum refertam . . ." etc.

Those ideas lead back to the "descent" or "fall of the deity" in the Gnostic systems (cf. W. W. Bussell, *Religious Thought and Heresy in the Middle Ages* [1918], p. 554 *et sqq.*). Reitzenstein, *Poimandres* (1904), p. 50; G. R. S. Mead, *Pistis Sophia* (1921), p. 36 *et sqq.; idem, Fragments of a Faith Forgotten* (2d ed., 1906), p. 470.

22. "Est in mari piscis rotundus, ossibus et corticibus carens, et habet in se pinguedinem" (= humidum radicale = anima mundi enclosed in matter) ("Allegoriae super Turbam," *Art. Aurif.* [1593], I, 141).

23. *Timaeus*, p. 7.

24. Cf. Note 21.

25. "Nam ut coelum, quoad visibile, . . . rotundum in forma et motu, . . . sic Aurum" (M. Majer, *De Circulo*, p. 39).

26. "Rosarium Philosophorum" (in *Art. Aurif.*, etc. [1593], II, 261). The tract is ascribed to Petrus Toletanus, who lived in Toledo about the middle of the thirteenth century. He is said to be either an older contemporary, or a brother of Arnaldus de Villanova, the famous physician and "philosopher." The actual form of the "Rosarium," based upon the first print from 1550, is a compilation and probably does not date back further than the fifteenth century, though certain parts may have originated in the early thirteenth century.

27. *Symposium* XIV.

28. Petrus Bonus in Janus Lacinius, *Pretiosa Margarita Novella*, etc. (1546). Reprinted in *Theatr. Chem.* (1622), p. 567 *et sqq.* and in J. J. Mangeti, *Bibl. Chem.*, II (1702), 1 *et sqq.* Concerning the allegoria Christi cf. "Erlösungsvorstellungen," etc., *Eranos-Jahrbuch 1936*, p. 82 *et sqq.*

29. Beati Thomae de Aquino, *Aurora sive Aurea Hora.* Complete text in the rare print of 1625, *Harmoniae Imperscrutabilis Chymico-Philosophicae sive Philosophorum Antiquorum Consentientium Decas I.* Francofurti apud Conrad Eifridum. Anno MDCXXV (Brit. Mus. Libr., 1033, d. 11). The interesting part of the tract is the first part, *Tractatus Parabolarum*, omitted on account of its "blasphemous" character in the prints of 1572 and 1593 in *Artis Auriferae*, etc. In the *Cod. Rhenovac.* of the Zentralbibliothek in Zürich, about four chapters of the *Tract. Parab.* are lacking. The *Cod. Parisin. Fond Latin* 14006, of the Bibliothèque Nationale, contains a complete text of the *Tract. Parab.*

30. A good example is contained in the commentary of D. Gnosius to *Tract. Aur. Hermetis* (Reprints in *Theatr. Chem.*, IV [1613], 672 *et sqq.* and in J. J. Mangeti, *Bibl. Chem.*, I [1702], 400 *et sqq.*).

31. In *Aurea Hora, loc. cit.*, see Note 29. Zosimos (περὶ ὀργάνων, Berthelot, *Alch. Grecs.*, III, XLIX, 4–5), quoting from a Hermetic writing, says that ὀθεοῦ υἱός πάντα γενόμενος is *Adam* or *Thot*, consisting of the four elements and the four directions of space.

32. In *Aurea Hora*, see Note 29. For Latin text, see III, Note 86.

33. "Erlösungsvorstell. i. d. Alchemie," *Eranos-Jahrbuch 1936*, p. 20 *et sqq.*

34. Charlotte A. Baynes, *A Coptic Gnostic Treatise contained in the Codex Brucianus* (Cambridge, 1933), pp. 22, 89, 94.

35. "The Rosarium Philosophorum" (*Art. Aurif.*, II, 204 *et sqq.*), being one of the first synoptic attempts, gives a sufficiently comprehensive account of the medieval quaternity.

36. Cf. the palaeolithic (?) "Sun Wheels" of Rhodesia.

37. I do not refer to the dogma of the human nature of Christ.

38. I refer chiefly to works containing alchemistic legends (Lehrerzählungen). A good example is M. Majer, *Symbola aureae mensae duodecim nationum* (1617), containing the symbolic peregrinatio, p. 569 *et sqq.*

39. As far as I know there are no complaints in alchemistic literature of persecution by the church. The authors allude usually

to the tremendous secret of the magisterium as a reason for secrecy.

40. See *Pandora*, 1588 (the glorification of the body in the form of an assumption of Mary). St. Augustine has also symbolized the Virgin by the earth: "Veritas de terra orta est, quia Christus de virgine natus est" (*Sermones*, 188, I, 5, p. 890). The same Tertullian, "Illa terra virgo nondum pluviis rigata nec imbribus foecundata . . ." (*Adv. Iud.*, 13, p. 199 A).

III

1. *Psychology of the Unconscious.*

2. A repetition of the old symbol of the οὐροβόρος, the "tail-eater."

3. An Eastern parallel is the "circulation of the light" in a Chinese Alchemistic tract, *The Secret of the Golden Flower*, edited by R. Wilhelm and myself.

4. Wallis Budge, *Osiris and the Egyptian Resurrection*, I, 3; *idem, Book of the Dead*, facsimile, 1899, Pl. 5. In a manuscript of the seventh century (Gellone) the evangelists are represented with the heads of their symbolic animals instead of human heads.

5. An example in *Secret of the Golden Flower*.

6. Kazi Dawa-Samdup, "Shrîchakrasambhâra Tantra," *Tantric Texts*, ed. Arthur Avalon, Vol. VII (1919).

7. Abbé Joseph Delacotte, *Guillaume de Digulleville. Trois Romans-Poèmes du XIVe Siècle* (Paris, 1932).

8. See R. Eisler, *Weltenmantel und Himmelszelt*, I, 85 *et seq.*

9. See Zeller, *Griech. Phil.*, III Th., p. 120. According to Archytas the soul is a circle or ball.

10. See the invocations in the "Acts of Thomas" (Mead, *Fragments*, p. 422 *seq.*)

11. With the Gnostics the quaternity is decidedly female. See Irenaeus, *Advers. Haer.*, cap. XI.

12. See Definitions 48 and 49 in *Psychological Types*, p. 588 *et sqq.*

13. A special case is the so-called "inferior function." See Definition 30 in *Psychological Types*, p. 563 *et sqq.*

14. Concerning the assimilation of the "shadow," see *Psychological Types*, p. 203.

15. See Mead, *Fragments*, p. 231. The same exegesis in *Pistis Sophia* (see Carl Schmidt, *Pistis Sophia* [1925], p. 215).

16. In Thibetan Buddhism the four colors are connected with

psychological qualities (four forms of wisdom) (see Evans-Wentz, *The Tibetan Book of the Dead* [1927], p. 104 *et sqq.*).

17. See Definition 51 in *Psychological Types*, p. 601.

18. Concerning the psychology of the mandala, see *Secret of the Golden Flower* (1931), p. 96 *et sqq.*

19. See Definition 46 in *Psychological Types*, p. 585.

20. See Hauer, "Symbole und Erfahrung des Selbstes in der Indo-Arischen Mystik," *Eranos-Jahrbuch 1934*, p. 35.

21. About the concept of "relativity of God," see *Psychological Types*, p. 297 *et sqq.*

22. This fact accounts for the theory of Animism.

23. Concerning the concept of "inflation," see *Two Essays*, p. 145 *et sqq.*

24. Berthelot, *Alch. Grecs.*, IV, XX. According to F. Sherwood Taylor, "A Survey of Greek Alchemy," *Journ. of Hellenist. Stud.*, L, 109 *et sqq.*, probably the oldest Greek text of the first century. See also J. Hammer Jensen, *Die älteste Alchemie* (1921).

25. Berthelot, *Alch. Grecs.*, III, I, *et sqq.*

26. Scott, *Hermetica* (1924).

27. Berthelot, *Alch. Grecs.*, II, I, *et sqq.*

28. Early in the Greek alchemists, we already encounter the idea of the "stone that contains a spirit" (cf. Berthelot, *Alch. Grecs.*, III, VI). The "stone" is the prima materia, called Hyle or Chaos or massa confusa. This alchemistic terminology was based upon Plato's *Timaeus*. Thus J. Ch. Steebus (*Coelum Sephiroti-cum*, etc. [1679]) quotes (p. 26): "materia prima quae receptaculum et mater esse debit ejus quod factum est et quod videri potest, nec terra, nec aer, nec ignis, nec aqua debet dici, nec quae ex his, neque ex quibus haec facta sunt, sed species quaedam, quae videri non potest et informis est et omnia suscipit." The same author (*ibid.*) calls the prima materia also "primaeva terra chaotica, Hyle, Chaos, abyssus, mater rerum. . . . Prima illa chaotica materia. . . . Coeli influentis humectata, insuper a Deo innumerabilibus specierum Ideis exornata fuit. . . ." He explains how the spirit of God descended into matter and what became of him there (p. 33): "Spiritum Dei aquas superiores singulari fotu faecundasse et velut lacteas effecisse. . . . Produxit ergo spiritus sarcti fotus in aquis supracoelestibus [according to Gen. I.6 *et seq.*] virtutem omnia subtilissime penetrantem et foventem, quae cum luce combinans, in inferiorum Regno minerali serpentem mercurii [which refers just as well to the caduceus of Aesculapius, since the serpent is also the origin of the "medicina catholica," the panacea], in

vegetabili benedictam viriditatem [the chlorophyll], in animali plasticam virtutem progenerat, sic ut spiritus supracoelestis aquarum cum luce maritatus, anima mundi merito appellari possit" (p. 38). "Aquae inferiores tenebricosae sunt, et luminis effluvia intra sinuum capacitates absorbent." This doctrine is based upon nothing less than the Gnostic legend of the nous descending from the higher spheres and being caught in the embrace of the physis. The mercurius of the alchemists is a "volatile." Abu'l-Qāsim Muhammad (Kitāb al'ilm al muktasab, etc., thirteenth century, ed. E. J. Holmyard [1923]) speaks of "Hermes, the volatile" (p. 37), and in many places mercury is called a "spiritus." Moreover, he was understood to be a Hermes psychopompos, showing the way to Paradise (see M. Majer, Symb. aur. mens., p. 592). This is very much the role of a redeemer, attributed to the νοῦς in Ἑρμοῦ πρὸς Τάτ (Scott, Hermetica, I, 149 et sqq.). With the Pythagoreans the soul is entirely devoured by matter, with the sole exception of reason (see Zeller, Griech. Phil., III Th., p. 158).

In the old Commentariolus in Tabulam Smaragdinam, Hortulanus speaks of the "massa confusa" or the "chaos confusum," from which the world was created and from which also the mystical lapis issues. The latter was identified with Christ from the beginning of the fourteenth century (Petrus Bonus, 1330). The Epilogus Orthelii (Theatr. Chem., VI, 431) says: "Salvator noster Christus Jesus . . . duarum naturarum particeps est: Ita quoque terrenus iste salvator ex duabus partibus constat scl. coelesti et terrestri. . . ." In the same way the mercurius imprisoned in matter was identified with the Holy Ghost, Joh. Grasseus (in "Arca Arcani," Theatr. Chem., VI, 314) quotes: "Spiritus sancti donum, hoc est plumbum Philosophorum, quod plumbum aeris appellant, in quo splendida columba alba inest, quae sal metallorum vocatur, in quo magisterium operis consistit."

Concerning the extraction and transformation of the chaos, Christopher of Paris ("Elucidarius," Theatr. Chem., VI, 228) says: "In hoc chaote profecto in potentia existit dicta pretiosa substantia natura in una elementorum unitorum massa confusa. Ideoque ratio humana in id incumbere debet ut coelum nostrum ad actum deducat." "Coelum nostrum" refers to the microcosm and is also called "quinta essentia." Coelum is the incorruptibile and immaculatum. Johannes de Rupescissa (La Vertu et la Propriété de la Quinte Essence [Lyon, 1581], p. 18) calls it "le ciel humain." It is evident that the philosophers transferred the vision of the golden and blue circle to their aurum philosophicum (which was called "rotundum," see M. Majer, *De Circulo*, p. 15) and to their blue quintessence.

The terms chaos, massa confusa were, according to the testimony of Bernardus Silvestris, a contemporary of William of Champeaux (1070–1121), in general use. His work, *De Mundi Universitate Libri duo sive Megacosmus et Microcosmus* (ed. C. S. Barach and J. Wrobel [Innsbruck, 1876]) had a widespread influence. "Primae materiae, id est hyles, confusio" (pp. 5, 18). "Silva regens, informe chaos concretio pugnax
"Discolor usiae vultus, sibi dissona massa . . ." (pp. 7, 18)
"Massa confusionis" (pp. 56, 10) Bernardus mentions also the descensus spiritus in the following way:

> "Coniugis in gremium Jove descendente movetur,
> Mundus et in partum urgeat omnis humum."

Another variant is the idea of the King submerged or concealed in the sea (M. Majer, *Symb. aur. mens.*, p. 380; Visio Arislei, *Art. Aurif.*, I, 146 *et sqq.*).

29. For instance, the genius of the planet Mercury reveals the secrets to Pseudo-Demokritos (Berthelot, *Alch. Grecs.*, I, 236).

30. J. de Rupescissa, *La Vertu*, etc., p. 19.

31. Djābir in the *Book of Compassion* says that the Philosopher's Stone is equal to a microcosm (Berthelot, *La Chimie au Moyen Âge*, I, III, p. 179).

32. It is difficult not to assume that the alchemists were greatly influenced by the allegorical style of the patristic literature. They even claim certain Fathers as representatives of the Royal Art, for instance Albertus Magnus, Thomas Aquinas, Alanus de Insulis, etc. A text like the *Aurea Hora* or *Aurora Consurgens* is full of allegorical interpretations of the scriptures. It is attributed even to Thomas Aquinas. Water was used, however, as allegoria spiritus sancti: "Aqua viva gratia Sp. S." (Rupert abb. Migne, *Patrolog. Curs. Compl.*, CLXIX, 353); "Aqua fluenta Sp. S." (S. Bruno Herbipol, *loc. cit.*, CXLII, 293); "Aqua S. Sp. infusio" (Garner. de S. Victore, *loc. cit.*, CXCIII, 279). Water is also an allegoria humanitatis Christi (S. Gaudentius, *loc. cit.*, XX, 985). Very often water appears as dew (ros Gedeonis). Dew is also an allegoria Christi: "ros in igne visus est" (S. Roman, *De Theophania;* J. B. Pitra, *Analecta sacra*, etc. [Paris, 1876], I, 21). "Nunc in terra ros Gedeonis fluxit" (S. Roman, *loc. cit.*, p. 237).

The alchemists assumed the aqua permanens to be gifted with a virtue which they called "flower" (flos). It had the effect of transforming a body into spirit, and of giving an incorruptible quality to it (*Turba Philosophorum*, ed. Ruska [1931], p. 197). The water was also called acetum, "quo Deus perficit opus, quo et corpora spiritus capiunt et spiritualia fiunt" (*Turba*, p. 126). Another name is "spiritualis sanguis" (*Turba*, p. 129). The *Turba* is an early Latin tract of the twelfth century, translated from an original Arabic composition of the ninth–tenth centuries (Ruska). Its contents, however, are derived from Hellenistic sources. The Christian allusion in spiritualis sanguis could be due to Byzantine influence. The aqua perm. is mercury, argentum vivum (Hg). "Argentum vivum nostrum est aqua clarissima nostra" ("Rosarium Philosophorum," *Art: Aurif.*, II, 213). The aqua is also called "fire" (ignis, *idem*, p. 218). The body is transformed by water and fire, a complete parallel to the Christian idea of baptism and spiritual transformation.

33. Missale Romanum. The rite is old and known as benedictio minor (or major) salis et aquae since about the eighth century.

34. In "Isis, the Prophetess to Her Son" (Berthelot, *Alch. Grecs.*, I, XII, 1 *et sqq.*) an angel brings Isis a small vessel filled with transparent water, the arcanum. This is an obvious parallel to the κρατήρ of Hermes ('Ερμοῦ πρὸς Τάτ, *Corp. Herm.*) and the same of Zosimos (Berthelot, *Alch. Grecs.*, II, LI, 8) where the contents are νοῦς. In Pseudo-Demokritos' φυσικὰ καὶ μυστικά (Berthelot, *Alch. Grecs.*, I, 65) the divine water is said to bring about transformation by leading the "hidden nature" to the surface. In the tract of Komarios we find the miraculous waters that produce a new spring (Berthelot, *loc. cit.*, II, 281).

35. Gnosius (in *Hermetis Trismegisti Tractatus vere Aureus*, etc., *cum Scholiis Dominici Gnosii*, 1610, pp. 44 and 101) speaks of the "Hermaphroditus noster Adamicus," when he deals with the quaternity in the circle. The center is "mediator pacem faciens inter inimicos," clearly a *reconciling symbol* (see *Psychological Types*, p. 264 *et sqq.*). The hermaphrodite is derived from the "draco se ipsum impraegnans" (see *Art. Aurif.*, I, 303), mercury, the anima mundi. M. Majer, *Symb. aur. mens.*, p. 43, quotes the "doctrina Brachmanorum" in dealing with Apollonius of Tyana; see also Berthelot, *Alch. Grecs.*, I, 87. The οὐροβόρος is a hermaphroditic symbol. The hermaphrodite is also called Rebis ("made of two"), often represented through an apotheosis (for instance in "Rosarium Philosophorum," *Art. Aurif.*, II, pp. 291 and 359; the same in *Pandora* [1588], pp. 253).

36. The *Aurea Hora* (Pt. I) says, quoting Senior, "Est unum quod nunquam moritur, quoniam augmentatione perpetua perse-

verat; *cum corpus glorificatum fuerit in resurrectione novissima mortuorum.* . . . Tunc *Adam secundus* dicet priori et filiis suis: Venite benedicti patris mei," etc. (*Cod. Rhenovac,* Zentralbibl., Zürich).

37. For instance Alphidius: "Lux moderna ab eis gignitur, cui nulla lux similis est per totum mundum" ("Rosarium Philosophorum," *Art. Aurif.,* II, 248; the same Hermes, *Tract. Aur.*).

38. *Secret of the Golden Flower.*

39. See A. E. Waite, *The Secret Tradition in Alchemy* (1926).

40. *Psychological Factors Determining Human Behavior.* Harvard Tercentenary Publications, 1936.